Jacques Pepin
Chef

Susie Heller
Project Coordinator

The Cleveland Clinic Foundation

Dr. Michael Cressman
Director
Lipid Research Clinic

Sally Eyerdam, R.D.
Director
Nutrition Services

Susan Comfort
Nutrition Services

Karen Miller-Kovach, R.D.
Nutrition Services

A CLEVELAND CLINIC COOKBOOK

A FARE FOR THE HEART

LOW SODIUM, LOW FAT, LOW CHOLESTEROL

Recipes created by internationally recognized Chef Jacques Pepin
with the world-renowned Cleveland Clinic Foundation.

Before starting this or any other diet, please consult your physician.

Acknowledgments
The Cleveland Clinic Foundation
Department of Nutrition Services

Cookbook produced by the
Division of Public Affairs and
Corporate Development

CLINITEC, Inc.
10465 Carnegie Avenue
Cleveland, Ohio 44106

Library of Congress
Catalog Card Number 87-73510

ISBN 0-945504-00-4

First Edition

Table of Contents

Introduction

Who ever said healthy eating had to be ho-hum? The recipes in this cookbook were created by experts in cooking, nutrition and medicine who believe the secret to healthy eating is not simply saying "no" to fat, cholesterol and sodium, or modifying familiar favorites into tasteless imitations. Instead, these recipes show you how to "take it to the limit" without compromising healthy guidelines.

All the recipes meet the dietary guidelines for healthy heart nutrition as advocated by the National Cholesterol Education Program, the American Heart Association and the U.S. Guidelines for Healthy Americans. In addition, a complete nutritional profile of each recipe, including fat, calories, cholesterol and sodium content, is included in the index.

By mixing and matching recipes, you can create exciting and flavorful dinner menus that fit your lifestyle—from casual meals to elegant dining. There's no need to check the ingredients—the book has been designed so that you can choose any combination of appetizer, soup, salad, main course, side dish and dessert in single-serving portions and still be within the acceptable guidelines.

Enjoy!

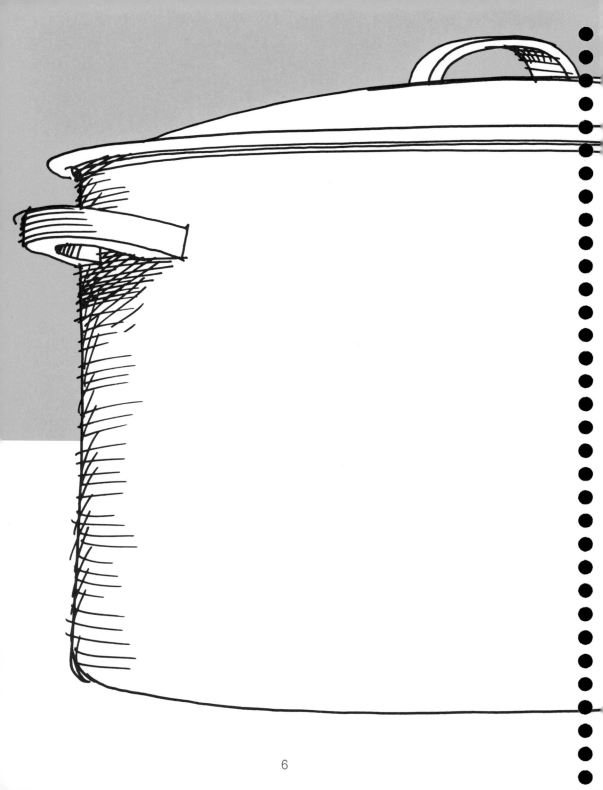

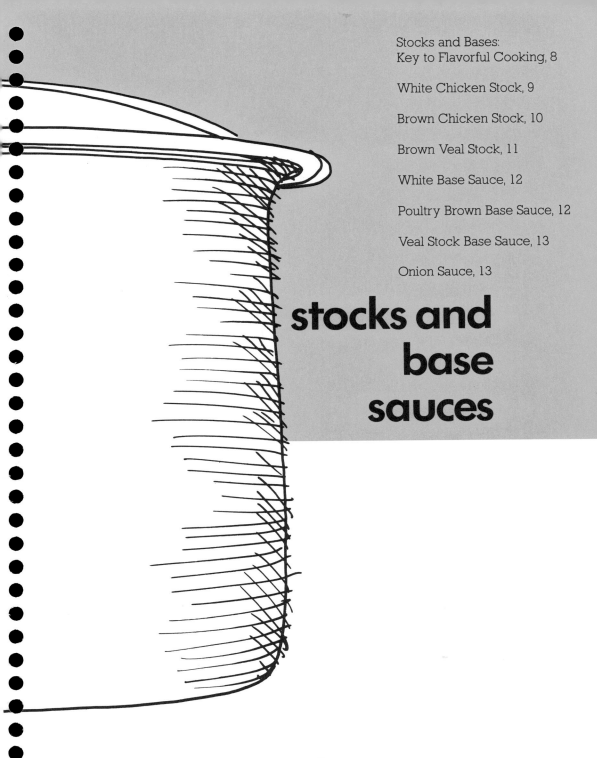

stocks and base sauces

Stocks and Bases: Key to Flavorful Cooking

The base sauces in this book, created from a variety of stocks, are very important. The stocks are made without salt and are skimmed as they cool to remove fat. This creates highly gelatinous stocks that freeze well.

Reducing stock produces a concentrate that can be used in sauces. For example, the Poultry Brown Base Sauce (see page 12), the Onion Sauce (see page 13) and the White Sauce (see page 12) are all made with reduced Chicken Stocks (see pages 9 and 10). Note: The Poultry Brown Base Sauce can be used interchangeably with the Veal Stock Base Sauce.

The sauces make great additions to most dishes. Since they have a strong, concentrated taste and give body and flavor, they are good in dressings, stews or with sautéed meats.

White Chicken Stock

Place the chicken bones and cold water into a large stockpot. Boil gently for 1 hour, removing any impurities and fat that rise to the top. Add the remaining ingredients and boil gently another 3 hours. Strain the stock through a fine strainer. Refrigerate the stock overnight. The next day, skim off any solidified fat that rises to the surface. Measure the stock. You should have 2 1/2 gallons. If you have more, return the stock to the stove and reduce it to 2 1/2 gallons. If you have less, add additional water to make 2 1/2 gallons. Freeze or refrigerate the stock and use as needed.

Must be refrigerated overnight.

Yield: 2 1/2 gallons

5 pounds chicken bones

1 large onion (3/4 pound)

4 large stalks celery - washed, trimmed and cut into chunks (1 pound)

3 large carrots - washed and cut into chunks (1/2 pound)

1 bay leaf

1 teaspoon black peppercorns

3 1/2 gallons cold water

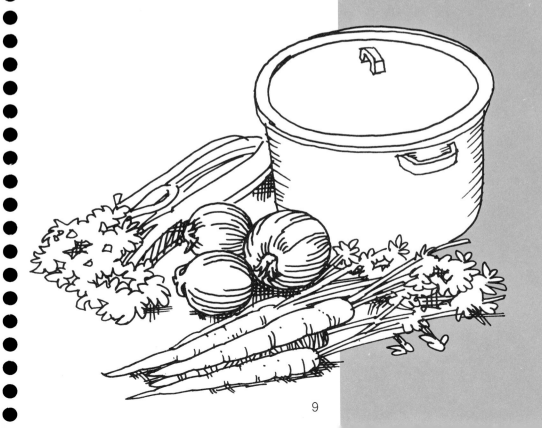

Must be refrigerated overnight.

Yield: 2 gallons/1 quart

15 pounds chicken bones

3 medium onions, quartered (2 pounds)

4 large stalks celery - washed, trimmed and cut into chunks (1 pound)

6 large carrots - washed and cut into chunks (1 pound)

2 bay leaves

1 teaspoon thyme leaves

2 teaspoons black peppercorns

3 1/2 gallons of water

Brown Chicken Stock

Preheat the oven to 400 degrees. Place the chicken bones in a large roasting pan and bake for 1 hour. Add the onions and carrots to the pan and bake for an additional 30-45 minutes or until the bones are well browned.

Using a slotted spoon, transfer the bones and vegetables to a large stockpot. Drain the accumulated fat from the roasting pan. Pour 2 cups of water into the pan; place on top of stove; bring to a boil and rub the bottom of the pan with a flat wooden spatula to melt all the solidified juices. Add this liquid and the remaining water to the stockpot.

Boil gently for 1 hour, removing any impurities and fat that rise to the top. Add the celery, bay leaves, thyme and peppercorns. Boil the stock gently for 5 more hours. Strain through a fine strainer. Place the stock in the refrigerator and chill overnight.

The next day, skim off any solidified fat that rises to the surface. Measure the stock. It should yield 2 gallons plus 1 quart. If there is extra, return the stock to the stove and boil until reduced to the correct amount. If the yield is less than 2 gallons plus one quart, add water. Freeze or refrigerate the stock and use it as needed.

Brown Veal Stock

Must be refrigerated overnight.

Yield: 1 gallon

Preheat the oven to 400 degrees. Place the veal bones in a large roasting pan and bake for 1 hour. Add the onions and carrots to the pan and bake for an additional 30-45 minutes or until the bones are well browned.

Using a slotted spoon, transfer the bones and vegetables to a large stockpot. Drain the accumulated fat from the roasting pan. Pour 2 cups of water into the pan; place on top of stove; bring to a boil and rub the bottom of the pan with a flat wooden spatula to melt all solidified juices. Add this liquid and the remaining water to the stockpot.

Boil gently for 1 hour, removing any impurities and fat that rise to the top. Add the celery, bay leaves and peppercorns. Boil the stock gently for 5 more hours. Strain through a fine strainer. Place the stock in the refrigerator and chill overnight.

The next day, skim off any solidified fat that rises to the surface. Measure the stock. It should yield 1 gallon. If there's more than 1 gallon, return the stock to the stove and boil until the mixture reduces to 1 gallon. If the yield is less than 1 gallon, add water to make 1 gallon. Freeze or refrigerate the stock and use as needed.

12 pounds veal bones

3 medium onions, quartered (2 pounds)

4 large stalks celery - washed, trimmed and cut into chunks (1 pound)

6 large carrots - washed and cut into chunks (1 pound)

2 bay leaves

2 teaspoons black peppercorns

3 1/2 gallons water

White Base Sauce

Yield: about 3 cups

1 quart White Chicken Stock
(see page 9)

1 1/2 tablespoons cornstarch

2 tablespoons cold water

3/4 cup evaporated skim milk

Boil the chicken stock until the liquid is reduced to 2 cups. Mix together the cornstarch and water and whisk into the boiling stock. Add milk and whisk until the mixture is combined and thickened.

Poultry Brown Base Sauce

Yield: 1 cup

1 quart Brown Chicken Stock
(see page 10)

1 teaspoon cornstarch

1 tablespoon cold water

Boil the chicken stock until it is reduced to 1 cup. In a small bowl, mix the cornstarch and water and add to the boiling stock to thicken it.

Veal Stock Base Sauce

Boil the veal stock until the liquid is reduced to 2 cups. Mix together the cornstarch and water and whisk into the boiling stock. Stir until the mixture is thickened.

Yield: about 2 cups

1 quart Brown Veal Stock (see page 11)

1 1/2 tablespoons cornstarch

1/3 cup cold water

Onion Sauce

Place the onions in the food processor or blender and purée. Pour into a bowl and add the base sauce. Mix to combine.

Yield: 1 1/2 cups

6 ounces caramelized onions
(see Onion Papillote recipe, page 67)

1 cup Poultry Brown Base Sauce or Veal Stock Base Sauce

soups

3 large cucumbers, (3 pounds), peeled and seeded

4 tomatoes (1 1/2 pounds), cored, cut in half and seeded

1 medium green pepper (5 ounces), cored and seeded

6 ounces onion, peeled (1 1/2 cups)

2 slices bread, cut into 1/2-inch dice and browned in oven

4 cloves garlic

2 teaspoons jalapeño pepper, seeded and chopped

1/2 teaspoon fresh ginger, chopped

1/4 teaspoon freshly ground black pepper

1/2 cup water

2 tablespoons vinegar

1 tablespoon olive oil

2 cups unsalted tomato juice

3/4 teaspoon Tabasco sauce

1/4 teaspoon salt

1/2 teaspoon sugar

Gazpacho

Gazpacho is the ideal hot weather soup, combining fresh vegetables from the garden.

For the garnish:
Dice 1 cup each of cucumber, tomato and onion into 1/2-inch pieces, plus 1/2 cup green pepper diced into 1/4-inch pieces. Set aside along with the bread croutons.

For the gazpacho:
Coarsely chop the remaining cucumber, tomato, green pepper and onion and place in a blender along with the garlic, jalapeño pepper, ginger, black pepper and water. Blend until smooth, then add the vinegar, olive oil, tomato juice, Tabasco, salt and sugar. Blend again to combine. To serve, ladle the soup into bowls and let the guests help themselves to the garnishes or serve the soup garnished.

Cold Peach Soup

Cold peach soup can be served as a soup or as a dessert sauce poured directly over slices of pound cake.

Place the water, cloves, sugar and cinnamon in a small kettle and bring to a boil. Let simmer for 10 minutes and add the dissolved cornstarch, stirring with a whisk to blend it with the syrup. Bring the syrup to a boil again and set aside to cool.

When cold, remove the cinnamon stick and cloves, add the wine to the syrup and refrigerate.

Clean the peaches and remove the skin with a knife or by dipping the peaches in boiling water for 30 seconds and then peeling. (The soup may also be made with unpeeled peaches, if desired.) Split the peaches lengthwise and remove the pits. Slice 2 cups of the nicest peaches and set aside for use as a garnish. Purée the remaining peaches in the blender and add to the cold syrup with the reserved peach slices. Refrigerate overnight or a few hours before serving.

To serve, fill individual bowls with the soup and garnish with blueberries.

Refrigerate overnight or a few hours before serving.

Yield: 8 servings

1 1/2 cups water

4 cloves

3/4 cup sugar

1 stick cinnamon, broken into small pieces

2 tablespoons cornstarch, dissolved in 1/4 cup cold water

1 1/2 cups dry white wine

3 1/2 pounds ripe peaches (about 12)

1 cup fresh blueberries

Soup

1 1/2 cups onions, diced

1 1/2 cups celery, diced
(including leafy part)

2 cups mixed scallions and leeks, sliced
and loosely packed

2/3 cup green pepper, seeded
and diced

1 1/2 cups carrots, diced

1 1/2 cups eggplant, unpeeled
and diced

1 1/2 cups butternut squash, peeled,
seeded and diced

1 cup kohlrabi, peeled and diced

1 1/2 cups potatoes, peeled and diced

1 1/2 cups zucchini, diced

1 cup string beans, cut into pieces

9 cups White Chicken Stock
(see page 9)

1 cup lettuce leaves

2 cups spinach leaves

Pistou

1 cup basil

1/2 cup parsley

6 cloves garlic

1/4 cup White Chicken Stock
(see page 9)

1/4 cup grated Parmesan cheese

Vegetable Soup with Basil Pistou

This soup can be done ahead using a variety of vegetables. Pistou, a sauce originating from southern France, is similar to Italian pesto. It is used here to season the soup, but could also be used to season pasta.

For the soup:

Combine the onions, celery, scallions, leeks, green pepper, carrots, eggplant, butternut squash, kohlrabi, potatoes, zucchini, string beans and chicken stock in a large pot. Bring to a boil, lower the heat, cover and simmer for 45 minutes. Add the lettuce and spinach and cook for another 15 minutes. Meanwhile, prepare the pistou.

For the pistou:

Purée the basil, parsley, garlic, chicken stock and Parmesan cheese in a food processor until smooth. Remove to a bowl and set aside.

When the soup is cooked, remove 6 cups and purée it in a food processor. Return this mixture to the remaining soup in the pot and stir. (This will add body to the soup.) To serve, ladle the hot soup into individual bowls and top each with 1 tablespoon of the pistou mixture.

Oatmeal Soup

This delicious soup can be made in just a few minutes. The oatmeal gives it a satisfying, fresh taste. If leeks are not available, scallions or a mixture of scallions and onions can be substituted. Herbs from the garden—parsley, tarragon, chervil, basil—make nice additions.

Heat the butter and oil in a large saucepan and, when hot, add the leeks. Cook 2-3 minutes over medium-to-high heat. Add the carrots, turnips, celery and chicken stock. Bring to a boil. Boil gently, covered half-way with a lid, for 20 minutes. Add the oatmeal and salt and cook another 5 minutes.

Yield: 8 servings

1 tablespoon unsalted butter

1 tablespoon peanut oil

2 large leeks (about 12 ounces), cleaned and thinly sliced (2 1/2 cups)

3 carrots (about 6 ounces), peeled and cut into 1/4-inch dice (1 cup)

2 medium turnips (about 6 ounces), peeled and cut into 1/4-inch slices (1 cup)

2 celery stalks (about 5 ounces), cleaned and thinly sliced (1 cup)

7 cups White Chicken Stock (see page 9)

1/2 cup quick-cooking oatmeal

1/4 teaspoon salt

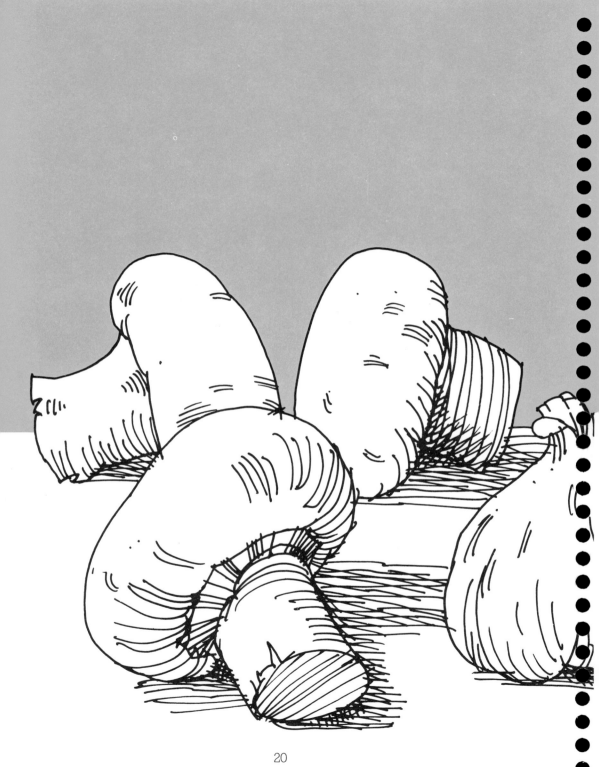

hors d'oeuvre

Crêpe Purse with Mushroom Duxelle, 22

Ratatouille Dip with Endive, 23

Egg Whites Stuffed with Bulgar, 24

Jalapeño Dip, 25

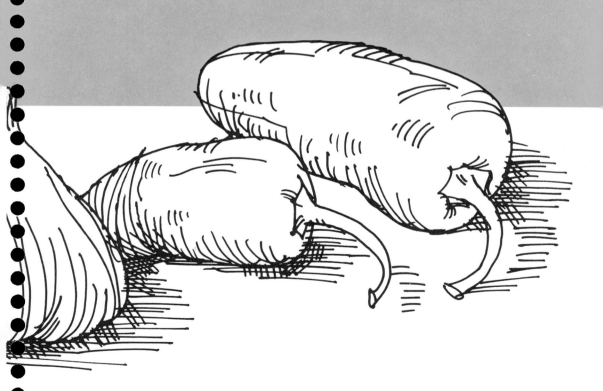

Crêpe Purse with Mushroom Duxelle

Yield: 8 servings

8 long strips scallion greens

1 tablespoon corn, safflower or sunflower oil

1/2 cup onion, chopped

1/3 cup pine nuts

2 pounds fresh domestic mushrooms, chopped in a food processor (about 3 cups)

1/4 cup chives, chopped

1/2 teaspoon Tabasco sauce

1/2 teaspoon sugar

1/4 teaspoon salt

8 shiitake mushrooms

1/4 cup water

1 tablespoon soy sauce

8 crêpes (see page 88)

This is an impressive dish for parties.

The crêpes are made with egg whites instead of whole eggs and are quite flavorful. The mixture of mushrooms, pine nuts and scallions makes a very satisfying crêpe filling. It also can be used as a stuffing for fish or meat.

Bring a small pot of water to a boil. Add the scallion greens and boil for about 10 seconds, until the greens are softened. Drain, pat dry and set aside.

Heat 2 teaspoons of the oil over medium-high heat in a non-stick skillet. When hot, add the onion and nuts and cook until the onion is softened and the nuts are browned. Add the chopped mushrooms and cook until the liquid evaporates, about 3 minutes. Toss in the chives and season with Tabasco, sugar and salt.

In a small skillet, heat the remaining 1 teaspoon oil over medium-high heat. When hot, add the shiitake mushrooms and the water, cover the pan and cook about 2 minutes. Remove the cover and continue to cook until all the water has evaporated and the mushrooms are browned. Brush the tops of the shiitake mushrooms with the soy sauce and cut each into thirds.

To serve: Arrange each crêpe in a small cup and fill the center with a heaping tablespoon of the mushroom duxelle. Bring up all sides of each crêpe and tie together at the top with a piece of scallion green. (The packets should resemble money sacks.) Put one sack on each plate and garnish the plates with pieces of the shiitake mushrooms.

Ratatouille Dip with Endive

Yield: 8 servings

Ratatouille, a classic dish from Provence, is a mixture of eggplant, zucchini, tomato, garlic and onion. Here, these ingredients are diced to create a dip.

Leaves of endive are used as "scoops" for the ratatouille, although it could be rolled in lettuce leaves. This dip is best served at room temperature or just slightly cooled.

Heat the oil in a saucepan until very hot. Add the onions and sauté over high heat for 3 minutes. Add the garlic, eggplant, jalapeño pepper, zucchini and 1/2 cup water. Cover the pan and boil gently for 10 minutes. Stir in the chopped tomato and bring back to a boil. Cook 10 minutes longer, then remove from heat. Set aside to cool. Mix together the white wine vinegar, salt and sugar and combine with the ratatouille.

To serve: Line each of 8 plates with a large piece of leaf lettuce and arrange 5 spears of endive in a star pattern around the edges of the plate. Place a 1/2-cup scoop of ratatouille in the center of each plate and garnish with a julienne of fresh basil. Serve with 3 toast triangles on each plate.

2 teaspoons corn, safflower or sunflower oil

1 10-ounce onion (2 1/2 cups), 1/2-inch dice

1 1/2 tablespoons garlic, chopped (6-7 cloves)

1 12-ounce eggplant (4 cups), 1/2-inch dice

2 teaspoons jalapeño pepper, seeded and chopped

1 8-ounce zucchini (2 cups), 1/2-inch dice

1/2 cup water

1 1/2 cups chopped tomatoes

2 tablespoons white wine vinegar

1/4 teaspoon salt

1/2 teaspoon sugar

8 large pieces leaf lettuce

40 spears Belgian endive

1/3 cup fresh basil, shredded

6 slices toasted bread, each cut into 4 triangles.

Egg Whites Stuffed with Bulgar

Yield: 10 servings

1 cup bulgar

3 cups water

1 tablespoon mint, finely chopped

1/2 cup parsley, finely chopped

1 teaspoon garlic, finely chopped (1-2 cloves)

1/3 cup scallions, chopped

1/2 teaspoon jalapeño pepper, seeded and finely chopped

1 cup tomatoes, peeled, seeded and diced (reserve peel)

2 teaspoons lemon peel, finely chopped

3 tablespoons fresh lemon juice

1/4 cup raisins

1/4 teaspoon Tabasco sauce

1/2 teaspoon salt

1 teaspoon sugar

15 hard-cooked eggs

This mixture of bulgar salad is accented with the taste of lemon juice and the sweetness of raisins.

For best flavor, it should be served at room temperature.

Cook the bulgar in water according to package directions. Add the mint, parsley, garlic, scallions, jalapeño pepper, tomatoes, lemon peel, lemon juice, raisins, Tabasco sauce, salt and sugar to the bulgar and mix well.

Cut the eggs in half lengthwise and discard the yolks. Fill each half with approximately 4 teaspoons of the filling. Julienne the reserved tomato peel and garnish each egg with a few strands.

Jalapeño Dip

Jalapeño pepper gives this dip a very spicy flavor. You can create hotter or milder versions by varying the amount of jalapeño added. The mixture will develop more flavor when refrigerated overnight.

Mix all ingredients together in a bowl. Serve with raw vegetables.

Best if refrigerated overnight.

Yield: 4 servings

1/2 cup tomato, seeded and chopped

1 tablespoon garlic, chopped (3-5 cloves)

1/2 teaspoon jalapeño pepper, seeded and chopped

1/3 cup fresh cilantro (coriander), chopped

3/4 cup mushrooms, cut into small cubes

3 tablespoons white wine vinegar

1 teaspoon chili powder

1 tablespoon sugar

2 tablespoons lemon juice

1/4 teaspoon Tabasco sauce

1/8 teaspoon salt

2 slices toasted bread, chopped finely

1 tablespoon corn, safflower or sunflower oil

Assorted fresh vegetables

salad dressings

Creamy French-Style Dressing

Yield: 2 cups
16 2-tablespoon servings, will dress
1 1/2 cups greens

1/2 cup tomato, peeled, seeded and chopped

1 teaspoon paprika

2 tablespoons scallions, chopped

1 1/2 teaspoons ginger, chopped

1/2 teaspoon freshly ground black pepper

2 teaspoons sugar

3 tablespoons balsamic vinegar

1 tablespoon red wine vinegar

3 tablespoons corn, safflower or sunflower oil

1 cup White Base Sauce (see page 12)

1 teaspoon dry mustard

1/2 teaspoon salt

This dressing gets its beautiful pink color from the paprika and fresh tomatoes. The balsamic vinegar gives it a distinctive taste.

A food processor or blender can be used to produce a creamier texture. If refrigerated, this dressing will keep for up to 10 days.

Combine all ingredients in a blender or food processor.

Creamy Cucumber Dressing

Yield: 2 cups
16 2-tablespoon servings, will dress
1 1/2 cups greens

3/4 cup cucumber, peeled, seeded and coarsely chopped

2 tablespoons dill

1 teaspoon jalapeño pepper, seeded

3 cloves garlic

2 tablespoons lemon juice

1 1/2 cups plain nonfat yogurt

2 tablespoons olive oil

1/2 teaspoon salt

2 teaspoons sugar

This cucumber dressing is flavored with garlic and lemon juice. Yogurt gives it a creamy texture and slightly sour taste, which is pleasantly offset by the sugar. The dressing is quickly and easily made using a blender to create a smoother texture than is possible with a food processor.

Place cucumber, dill, jalapeño and garlic in a blender and process until creamy. Mix with the remaining ingredients.

Vinaigrette Dressing

This vinaigrette dressing is accented with Brown Base Sauce (see page 12) and includes mustard, garlic, olive oil, parsley and red wine vinegar. The dressing develops more flavor after a few hours and can be kept, refrigerated, for up to 10 days.

Put all ingredients in a jar. Cover and shake.

Best if prepared several hours in advance.

Yield: 2 cups
16 2-tablespoon servings, will dress 1 1/2 cups greens

2 tablespoons Dijon mustard

1 teaspoon freshly ground black pepper

1 tablespoon garlic, chopped (3-5 cloves)

1/2 cup red wine vinegar

1 cup Poultry Brown Base Sauce (see page 12)

2 teaspoons parsley, chopped

1/4 cup olive oil

fish

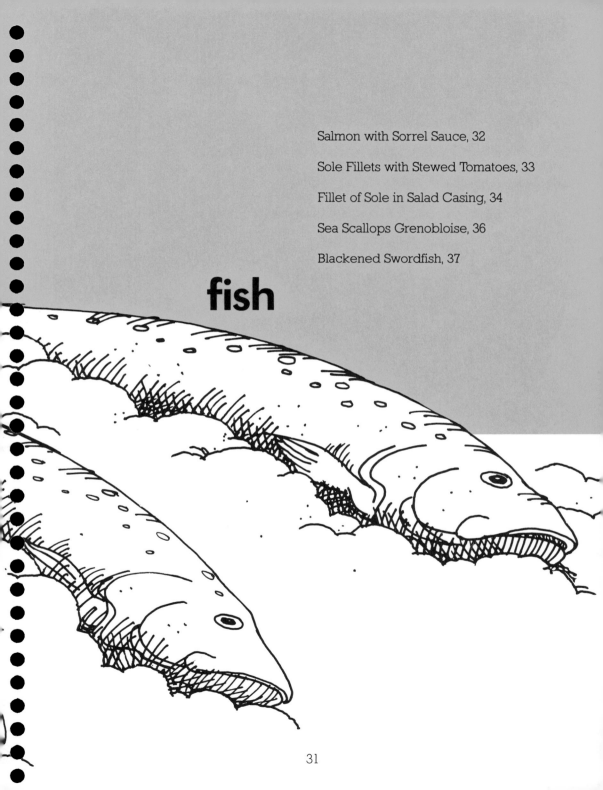

Salmon with Sorrel Sauce

Yield: 4 servings

4 6-ounce salmon fillets,
1/2-3/4 inch thick

1/2 cup white wine

8-10 large sorrel leaves, cut into a
chiffonade (see instructions)

1/2 cup White Base Sauce (see page 12)

1/4 teaspoon freshly
ground black pepper

1/2 teaspoon salt

The tart flavor of the sorrel cuts the richness of the fish and produces an excellent dish. If sorrel is not available, the same chiffonade mixture can be done with Boston lettuce leaves. If the lettuce is used, add 1/2 teaspoon lemon juice to the sauce just before serving to simulate the tartness of sorrel.

Place the salmon fillets and wine in a baking dish and bring to a boil on top of the stove. Place in a preheated 400-degree oven for 6-8 minutes.

Transfer the fish to a serving platter, cover with foil and keep warm while preparing the sauce.

Pour the juices from the baking pan into a saucepan and boil the liquid to reduce it to 2 tablespoons. Add the white sauce, pepper and sorrel and bring to a boil. Add salt and any juices that have accumulated around the fish.

Arrange the fish on a serving platter and pour the sauce over it. Serve immediately.

To make the chiffonade:
Stack the sorrel leaves together and roll them up tightly end to end. Cut crosswise with a sharp knife to get long, narrow strands.

Sole Fillets with Stewed Tomatoes

Yield: 8 servings

It's best to cook the fillets at the last moment and serve the dish as soon as it is ready.

Wash the chopped onions in a sieve under cold water to make them milder in flavor.

Arrange the fillets in a large gratin dish and sprinkle with the onions. Add the salt, white wine and tomatoes. Place a piece of waxed paper on top and bake in the center of a pre-heated 400-degree oven for 10-12 minutes. At that point, the fillets should be tender and just cooked through.

Remove the fillets to a serving platter. Pour the juice from the gratin dish into a skillet and boil to reduce to about 2/3 cup. Add the olive oil and bring the mixture to a boil. Immediately pour the sauce over the fillets and serve.

3/4 cup onion, very finely chopped

8 fillets of sole (5 ounces each)

1 teaspoon salt

3/4 cup dry white wine

1/2 cup tomatoes, peeled, seeded and diced

2 tablespoons olive oil

Yield: 4 servings

1 extra-large head iceberg lettuce (leafy-type)

6 ounces fresh mushrooms, finely chopped (about 2 cups loose)

1/2 teaspoon freshly ground white pepper

1/2 teaspoon salt

1 large carrot, peeled, sliced thin and julienned (1 cup loose)

1 leek, white and light green parts only, julienned (1 cup loose)

1 pound fillet of sole (about 4 ounces per person), each fillet split in half lengthwise and the small piece of bone between the halves removed

1 cup dry white wine

For the sauce:

2 tablespoons corn oil

1 tablespoon flour

cooking liquid from the fish

1/2 cup White Chicken Stock (see page 9)

a few drops of lemon juice, if desired

2 tablespoons parsley, chopped

Fillet of Sole in Salad Casing

Fillet of sole in salad casing is ideal for a party. The fish stays quite moist wrapped in the lettuce "packages."

Core the lettuce, then insert the tips of your fingers in the resulting hole and spread the leaves apart. This will help loosen the large outside leaves. Separate the leaves and pick out 8 of the largest ones. (Reserve the rest of the lettuce for another use.)

Drop the large leaves in boiling water, gently pushing them down into the water as they wilt. Bring the water back almost to a boil, at which point the leaves will be soft. Place the whole kettle under cold running water until the leaves are cold. Carefully lift the leaves out of the cold water and drain on paper towels.

Place the mushrooms in a skillet over medium heat and cook until all the liquid released from the mushrooms evaporates. Season with 1/4 teaspoon of the salt and put an equal amount of the finely chopped mushrooms on top of each lettuce leaf.

Sprinkle a large skillet with the remaining 1/4 teaspoon salt and 1/2 teaspoon of white pepper. Cover with the julienne of carrots and leeks.

Fold a single piece of fish and place over the mushroom mixture on each leaf. The white fleshy side of the fish should be on the outside or the fillets will unfold during cooking.

Fold the leaves over the fillets and place each package, seam-side-down, on top of the julienne of vegetables.

Pour the wine over the fillets and cover the skillet tightly with a lid. Bring to a boil and simmer gently for about 8 minutes, depending on how tightly the fillets are packed together. They can also be brought to a boil, then cooked in a preheated 425-degree oven for 8-10 minutes.

To make the sauce:

Heat the oil in a heavy saucepan and add the flour. Cook over medium heat for about 1 minute, stirring with a whisk. Holding the fillets in place with the lid, pour the cooking liquid from the fish into the oil-flour mixture. Mix carefully with a whisk, bring to a boil and whisk until the mixture thickens. Let simmer gently for about 5 minutes. You should have approximately 3/4 cup. Add the chicken stock, bring to a boil and allow to boil for 2-3 minutes, until the mixture is reduced to about 1 cup.

Remove the packages from the saucepan and arrange the julienne of vegetables on a serving platter.

Place the packages on top of the julienne and set in a 160-degree oven until ready to serve.

At serving time, pour out or blot up with paper towels any juices that have accumulated around the fillets so they will not thin down the sauce.

Heat the sauce, stirring in a few drops of lemon juice, if desired, and pour over the fillets. Sprinkle with the chopped parsley and serve immediately.

Sea Scallops Grenobloise

Yield: 4 servings

1 pound sea scallops

1 tablespoon water

1 tablespoon olive oil

1/2 teaspoon garlic, chopped (1 clove)

1 small zucchini, 1/4-inch dice (1 cup)

1 small red pepper, seeded and cut into 1/2-inch dice (3/4 cup)

1/4 teaspoon freshly ground pepper

1/8 teaspoon salt

1 lemon, skin removed, cut into 1/2-inch dice (1/3 cup)

2 pieces bread, cut into 1/2-inch dice and browned in the oven

1 tablespoon chives, chopped

The combination of colors makes this dish very attractive. For best results, be sure to add the croutons at the end. If added sooner, they tend to lose their crunchiness, which provides a nice contrast to the rest of the ingredients.

Place the scallops in a skillet with 1 table-spoon water. Bring to a boil, cover and cook 1 minute, until firm but still somewhat raw in the center. Remove the scallops and juices from the pan and keep them warm.

Heat the olive oil in a skillet over medium-high. When it is hot, add the garlic and sauté for 5-6 seconds. Then add the zucchini and red pepper and sauté 2-3 minutes. Add the drained scallops to the vegetables and season with the pepper and salt. Toss the ingredients together to warm and add the lemon.

Just before serving, add the bread croutons and sprinkle with the chives.

Blackened Swordfish

As in all our "sauté" recipes, we use a heavy, non-stick pan here. This is particularly important since almost no fat is used.

The mixture of thyme, oregano, cumin and especially the hotness of the black and cayenne peppers will coat the outside of the fish and give it a wonderful taste. The fish will be at its best if not cooked too long. A fish that is approximately 1-inch thick should be slightly undercooked in the center so it remains moist throughout.

Mix together all the dry ingredients and put on a plate.

Press the raw swordfish steaks into the mixture, coating them well on both sides.

Heat the oil in a non-stick skillet over high heat. When very hot, brown the fish for 1 minute on each side. Reduce the heat to low, cover and cook the fish an additional 4 minutes.

Sprinkle lemon juice over the fish and serve immediately.

Yield: 4 servings

1 tablespoon corn, safflower or sunflower oil

1 teaspoon dried thyme

1 teaspoon dried oregano

1/2 teaspoon cumin powder

1/2 teaspoon freshly ground black pepper

1/4 teaspoon cayenne pepper

1/4 teaspoon salt

4 6-ounce swordfish steaks

juice from 1 lemon

poultry

Yield: 6 servings

8 ounces dry white beans
(Navy, Great Northern)

1 large onion (about 6 ounces) studded
with 3 whole cloves

2 large carrots, peeled and cut into
1-inch pieces

1 stalk celery, sliced

1/2 teaspoon salt

1/4 teaspoon thyme

2 bay leaves

4 cups White Chicken Stock
(see page 9)

1/2 cup tomato, cored, seeded and
coarsely chopped

1 teaspoon garlic, chopped

1/4 cup fresh parsley, chopped

2 pounds boneless turkey steaks, cut
into strips about 2 inches long by
1/2-inch thick by 1/4-inch wide

A few drops of Tabasco sauce (optional)

Turkey Cassoulet

The cassoulet is an earthy dish from the southwest of France. Traditionally, it is made with white beans, poultry and meat or sausage. In our leaner, healthier version, we use breast of turkey, adding it at the end so the breast is not overcooked and stays moist. It is best to set the dish aside for a few minutes after cooking to let the flavors develop before serving. In addition, it tastes better if not served too hot.

Rinse the beans in a sieve under cold water, discarding any stones or damaged beans.

Place the beans in a large pot with the onion, carrots, celery, salt, thyme, bay leaves and stock. Bring to a boil, cover and boil very gently for 2 hours, stirring every 15-20 minutes to prevent the beans from sticking to the bottom of the pot. After 2 hours the beans should be tender and the liquid absorbed.

Remove the cloves and discard. Coarsely chop the onion and add with the tomato, garlic and parsley. Bring the dish back to a boil and simmer another 5 minutes. Add the turkey, bring to a boil and simmer for 2-5 minutes or until the turkey is opaque. Serve within the next hour.

Note: For additional flavor, sprinkle the finished dish with Tabasco to taste.

Chicken in Mustard Sauce

Yield: 8 servings

Chicken in mustard sauce can be prepared quickly and easily. It is quite flavorful and in-expensive. It is also good served cold or at room temperature for a buffet.

Sprinkle meat with the salt and pepper.

Heat the oil in a large skillet over medium-high heat. When it is hot, brown the chicken for 1 1/2 minutes on each side, until nicely browned.

Mix in the onion and keep cooking for 1 minute.

Sprinkle the flour on the chicken pieces, turning them so that all the pieces are coated. Cook 1 minute to lightly brown the flour.

Add the water and stir until the mixture comes to a boil. Lower the heat, cover the skillet and boil gently for 5 minutes.

Remove the meat to a serving platter and keep warm.

Cook the sauce to reduce it to about 1 1/2 cups. Mix the dry mustard with the Dijon mustard and stir until smooth. Stir the mustard mixture into the sauce and heat but do not allow the sauce to boil.

Place the chicken pieces in the sauce and keep over low heat for 10-15 minutes to develop the flavor.

Serve the chicken with the sauce.

8 5-ounce chicken breasts, skinless and boneless

1/2 teaspoon salt

1/2 teaspoon freshly ground black pepper

1 tablespoon corn, safflower or sunflower oil

1 cup onion, finely chopped

2 tablespoons flour

2 cups water

1 1/2 teaspoons dry mustard

1 tablespoon Dijon mustard

41

Chicken Sauce Piquant

Yield: 6 servings

6 chicken breasts, boned and skin removed (about 5 ounces each)

1 teaspoon dried oregano

2 tablespoons olive oil

3/4 teaspoon salt

3/4 teaspoon freshly ground black pepper

3-5 cloves garlic, peeled, crushed and finely chopped (1 tablespoon)

1/3 cup red wine vinegar

1 cup Brown Chicken Stock (see page 10)

2 tomatoes, peeled, seeded and coarsely chopped (about 1 1/2 cups)

1/4 teaspoon Tabasco sauce

1 1/2 teaspoons cornstarch dissolved in 1 tablespoon water (if needed)

2 tablespoons chives or tarragon, chopped

2 tablespoons parsley, chopped

This lively chicken dish gets its zip from a sauce accented with red wine vinegar, fresh tomato and Tabasco. These flavors blend well with the oregano and garlic. This is a good dish to serve at room temperature for a buffet.

Sprinkle the chicken with the oregano, 1 tablespoon of olive oil, salt and pepper. Allow to marinate at least 1 hour. Place the remaining tablespoon of olive oil in a large skillet and heat over medium-high. Add the pieces of chicken. (The skillet should not be too crowded.) Sauté for 1 1/2 minutes on each side. Transfer the chicken to a platter, cover and keep in a 180-degree oven.

Add the garlic to the saucepan and cook for about 30 seconds. Add the vinegar and bring to a strong boil. Reduce by boiling until almost all the liquid has evaporated. Add the chicken stock and tomato and bring to a boil. Simmer gently for 2-3 minutes. Add the dissolved cornstarch if the sauce is too thin. Season with Tabasco, add the pieces of chicken to the skillet and cook just long enough to heat through. Arrange on a platter, spoon sauce on top, sprinkle with the herbs and serve immediately.

Chicken African-Style

Chicken African-style is much better when the chicken marinates ahead with the different seasonings. Although our recipe indicates 4-5 hours of marinating, the chicken can be prepared in the marinade up to a day in advance of serving to enhance the flavor.

Cut the chicken into 6 pieces. For this recipe, legs, thighs and breast halves will be used. Reserve the wings and bones for stock and discard the skin.

Mix together the onion, garlic, pepper flakes, ginger, salt, pepper and lime juice. Let the chicken pieces marinate in the mixture, covered, overnight in the refrigerator or for 4-5 hours at room temperature, mixing every hour.

Heat the oil in a non-stick skillet and, when hot, brown the pieces of chicken on all sides. Place the chicken in a large kettle.

Discard any oil remaining in the skillet. Deglaze the skillet by adding the marinade and scraping up any solidified chicken juices clinging to the pan.

Pour the marinade over the chicken in the kettle, bring to a boil, cover and simmer slowly for 15 minutes. Then, take off the cover, remove the chicken pieces and boil the sauce over high heat for 5 minutes to reduce it, if necessary.

Pull the cooked meat off the chicken bones and shred it into long strips. Return the meat to the sauce, warm through and serve immediately over Couscous (see page 64).

Must be prepared several hours in advance.

Yield: 5 servings

1 4-pound chicken, skin removed

2 cups onion, very thinly sliced (2 large)

4-6 cloves garlic, peeled and finely chopped

1/2 teaspoon hot chili-pepper flakes

1/2 tablespoon ginger, freshly grated

1/2 teaspoon salt

1/4 teaspoon freshly ground black pepper

1/4 cup lime juice

2 tablespoons corn, safflower or sunflower oil

1 pound boneless, skinless chicken breast, trimmed of all excess fat and cut into 1 1/2-inch chunks

1 1/2 teaspoons cornstarch

1 egg white, lightly beaten

8 ounces broccoli

1 cup Brown Chicken Stock (see page 10)

4 teaspoons soy sauce

1/4 teaspoon hot red pepper flakes

1 1/2 tablespoons corn, safflower or sunflower oil

1/2 tablespoon Chinese sesame oil

1 1/4 cups sliced onion

3-4 cloves garlic, finely chopped

1 tablespoon peeled, freshly grated ginger

Chicken Stir-Fry

This dish is prepared very quickly in the Chinese method. Here, however, we use a non-stick skillet to cook the chicken. A mixture of cornstarch and egg white on the chunks of chicken gives it a light coating and delicate flavor. Pepper flakes, sesame oil, garlic and ginger give the dish a strong, accented taste that stands up well to the broccoli or other vegetables.

Mix the chicken chunks with 1 teaspoon of the cornstarch and add the lightly beaten egg white.

Cut the flowerets from the broccoli stalks and separate them into smaller pieces. Peel the stalks and slice them into long, narrow strips approximately 4 inches long by 1-inch wide by 1/4-inch thick.

Mix together the chicken stock, remaining 1/2 teaspoon cornstarch, soy sauce and pepper flakes. Set aside.

Heat both oils in a large skillet. When hot, add the chicken and cook 2 1/2 minutes, turning the pieces as they brown. Remove the chicken from the skillet and return the drippings to the pan. Add the onions and sauté for about 30 seconds. Add the broccoli pieces, cover the pan and cook for 2 minutes, stirring occasionally. Return the chicken to the pan and add the garlic and ginger. Stir the reserved chicken stock mixture into the pan and simmer for 2-3 minutes, until the chicken is heated through and the sauce is thickened. Serve immediately.

meats

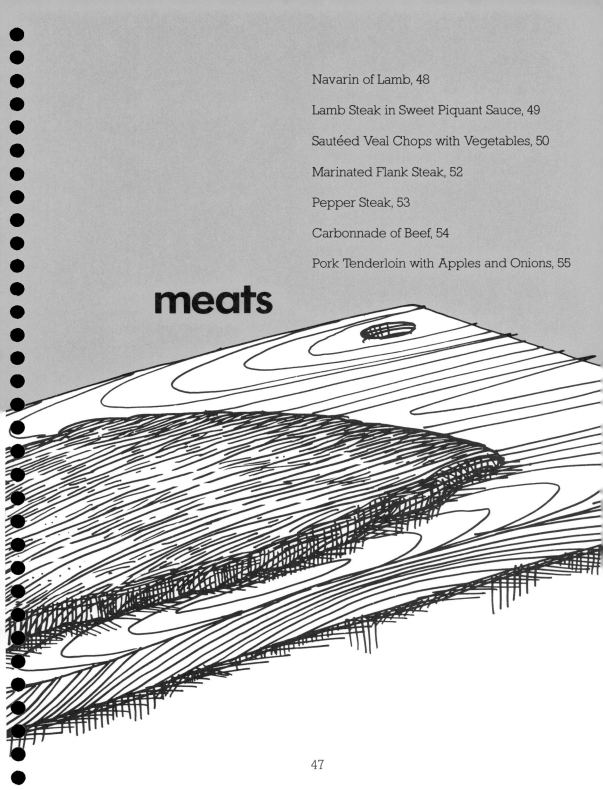

Best if meat prepared one day in advance and refrigerated.

Yield: 6 servings

2 tablespoons corn, safflower or sunflower oil

1 1/2 pound leg of lamb, trimmed of all visible fat and cut into 2-inch pieces

1 cup onions, sliced

1 tablespoon flour

about 2-3 cloves garlic, peeled and crushed (1 1/2 teaspoons)

3 cups water

1 teaspoon salt

1/2 teaspoon freshly ground black pepper

2 bay leaves

1 pound potatoes, peeled and cut into a 1 1/2-inch dice

2 carrots, cut into sticks

1 cup fresh peas, cooked in boiling water until tender or 1 cup frozen (without salt) peas (1/2 of a 12-ounce package)

Navarin of Lamb

Navarin of lamb is more flavorful if it is prepared ahead. The meat can be browned and cooked with the onions, garlic, water, flour and seasoning a day in advance. The potatoes, carrots and peas can then be added a few hours before serving. Other vegetables can be substituted, depending on the time of year.

Heat the oil in a large pot over high heat. When hot, add the lamb pieces, reduce the heat to medium and cook about 15 minutes, turning the pieces until they are browned all over. To remove the fat released from the meat, place a lid on top of the pot and, holding the lid with one hand and the pot by the handle, invert them over the sink and pour out the fat.

Add the onions to the meat in the pot and sauté for 1 minute over medium heat.

Add the flour, mix well and cook again for 1 minute. Then add the garlic, water, salt, pepper and bay leaves. Bring to a boil, cover and boil gently for 30 minutes.

Add the potatoes and carrots and boil gently for another 25 minutes.

Finally, add the peas and cook for 5 minutes longer.

Arrange the meat and vegetables on a large platter or individual plates and serve immediately while very hot.

Note: This stew doesn't have much sauce. The vegetables should be cooked until soft with the potatoes a bit mushy.

Lamb Steak in Sweet Piquant Sauce

The sweet-sour sauce served with lamb steaks here can also be used with Flank Steak (page 52), Pepper Steak (page 53) or with chicken breasts.

Pound each lamb steak to a 3/4-inch thickness and season on both sides with the pepper.

Heat the oil in a non-stick skillet over high heat until very hot. Add the lamb and cook about 1 1/2 minutes on each side.

Remove the lamb from the skillet and keep warm.

Add the vinegar and oregano to the skillet and cook to reduce the mixture to 2 tablespoons.

Add the Brown Base Sauce and currant jelly. Bring to a boil, add salt and any juice that has accumulated around the lamb and cook to reduce the mixture to 1/2 cup.

To serve, arrange the steaks on individual plates or cut the steaks into thin slices and serve with 2 tablespoons of the sauce.

Yield: 4 servings

4 lamb steaks cut from the leg, completely trimmed of fat, weighing 4 ounces each

1/2 teaspoon freshly ground black pepper

1 tablespoon corn, safflower or sunflower oil

1/3 cup white wine vinegar

1/2 teaspoon oregano

1/2 cup Poultry Brown Base Sauce (see page 12)

1/2 tablespoon currant jelly

1/2 teaspoon salt

Sautéed Veal Chops with Vegetables

For the veal chops:

6 boneless veal chops, trimmed, about 5-6 ounces each

1 tablespoon olive oil

1/2 teaspoon salt

For the vegetable garnish:

1/2 pound radishes (about 30), each cut in half

1/2 cup water

2 teaspoons olive oil

12 ounces large fresh mushrooms, cleaned and cut into 1/4-inch slices

2 medium-sized peppers (1 red, 1 green), about 5 ounces each, peeled with a vegetable peeler, seeded and cut into 12 strips each

1/4 teaspoon salt

The quality of the veal used for this dish is very important. Although the chops should be trimmed of all fat, a good quality veal— pink and plump—will give the best results. Notice that the veal is not cooked for very long, but is set aside to continue cooking in its own heat so it is cooked but not dry.

For the veal chops:

In a very large saucepan (or 2 smaller ones), heat the oil. Sprinkle the chops lightly with salt and cook over medium-to-high heat for 5 minutes on one side. Then turn and cook on the other side for 3 minutes. Cover and set aside for at least 15 minutes before serving. (Juices will come out of the chops and create a natural gravy.) Meanwhile, prepare the vegetables.

For the vegetable garnish:

Place the radishes in one layer in a stainless steel saucepan and add the 1/2 cup water. Bring to a boil and boil 4-5 minutes to soften slightly. (The radishes will still be crunchy.) Set aside.

Heat the oil in a skillet and, when hot, add the mushrooms. Sauté for about 3 minutes and add the pepper strips and salt. Sauté another minute and set aside.

Arrange the veal chops on individual plates and spoon some natural gravy on top. Place some of the radishes, mushrooms and peppers around the chops. Serve immediately.

Must marinate at least 2 hours or overnight.

Yield: 6 servings

1 1/2 pounds flank steak, trimmed of all visible fat

Marinade:

2 tablespoons honey

1 tablespoon vinegar

6 ounces onion, coarsely chopped

2 tablespoons soy sauce

2 cloves garlic

1 teaspoon jalapeño pepper, seeded and chopped

Marinated Flank Steak

Marinated flank steak is an excellent main dish. If the flank is not available, a skirt steak can be used and even a piece of top round will work, although it will be a bit dry if overcooked. All of these cuts are very lean.

Be sure to cut the cooked steak diagonally against the grain into thin slices. If served this way, the slices will be wider and more attractive and the meat very tender. If cut with the grain, however, the steak tends to be chewy and tough.

The marinade can also be used for chicken or to marinate pork.

Place the flank steak in a large plastic bag.

To make the marinade:

Blend the honey, vinegar, onion, soy sauce, garlic and jalapeño pepper in a food processor or blender.

Pour the mixture into the bag with the steak and marinate at least 2 hours or overnight.

Remove the steak from the bag (reserving the marinade) and grill or broil it for approximately 2 1/2 minutes per side or until medium rare. Pour the reserved marinade over the steak and let it rest for at least 15 minutes, uncovered, in a warm oven or on top of the stove or barbecue grill.

Slice the steak diagonally against the grain into thin slices. Serve immediately with the juices.

Pepper Steak

Yield: 2 servings

Pepper steak is excellent when done with freshly crushed black peppercorns. The Telli-cherry peppercorn or a similarly flavored, good quality variety gives the best results. The amount of pepper used depends on your own tastes and can be decreased or eliminated entirely.

Place the peppercorns on a cutting board and crush them by pressing with the back of a skillet in a forward rolling motion.

Press the crushed peppercorns into both sides of the steaks.

Heat the oil in a non-stick skillet until very hot. Add the steaks and sauté 1 1/2 minutes on each side. Remove the meat and keep warm while adding the garlic and red wine to the pan. Cook the liquid to reduce it to 1 tablespoon and add the onion sauce.

Season the steaks with the salt, arrange them on individual plates and pour some sauce over each. Serve immediately.

2 teaspoons fresh black peppercorns

2 5-ounce shell steaks, 1/2-inch thick, trimmed of all fat

1 teaspoon corn, safflower or sunflower oil

1/2 teaspoon garlic, minced

1/4 cup red wine

1/3 cup Onion Sauce (see page 13)

1/8 teaspoon salt

Best if prepared a day in advance.

Yield: 10 servings

2 1/2 pounds beef from round or chuck, (cut into 3-inch strips.)

3 tablespoons corn, safflower or sunflower oil

2 teaspoons salt

1 teaspoon freshly ground black pepper

6 tablespoons flour

3 cups onion, thickly sliced

1/3 teaspoon thyme

2 bay leaves

2 cans beer (or water or White Chicken Stock, see page 9)

Carbonnade of Beef

Carbonnade of beef is one of those earthy stews that will develop even more flavor if done ahead. The beer can be replaced with water if diet restrictions dictate or with White Chicken Stock (see page 9).

Heat the oil in a frying pan. When it sizzles, add half the meat, sprinkle it with 1 teaspoon of the salt and 1/2 teaspoon of the pepper and brown it lightly on all sides. Stir in 3 tablespoons of the flour and remove to a platter. Repeat this process with the remaining meat, salt, pepper and flour.

Brown the onions in the meat drippings.

Place a layer of the meat in a heavy pot. Cover with a layer of onions. Add another layer of meat, then onions. Repeat until all the meat and onions are used.

Arrange the thyme and bay leaves on top and cover with beer. The meat should be completely immersed. Bring to a boil, cover tightly and simmer for 1 1/2 hours. Serve with baked potatoes.

Pork Tenderloin with Apples and Onions

Yield: 4 servings

This dish with apples and onions uses the tenderloin, the leanest and most tender portion of pork. It should be trimmed of any sinew or fat, butterflied and pounded to a thickness of about 1/2 inch. The pork is only sautéed for a short time, but continues to cook in its own heat, which gives excellent results. The richness of the meat is also complemented by the tartness of the apples, vinegar and seasonings.

Season the pieces of pork on both sides with 1/2 teaspoon of pepper and thyme.

Heat the oil in a non-stick skillet over high heat until very hot. Add the pork to the pan and cook 2-3 minutes on each side. Remove the meat from the pan and keep it warm. Add the onion to the pan and sauté for about 3 minutes, until it is softened.

In a bowl, mix together the vinegar, water, sugar and cumin or caraway seeds and add to the pan along with the apples, salt and remaining 1/4 teaspoon pepper. Cover and boil gently 4-5 minutes, until the liquid has almost evaporated and the apples are moist and tender. Return the pork steaks and any accumulated juices to the pan and reheat for 1-2 minutes. Serve.

4 4-ounce pieces pork tenderloin, completely trimmed of fat, butterflied, and pounded to a thickness of 1/2 inch

3/4 teaspoon freshly ground black pepper

1/4 teaspoon crushed dry thyme

1 tablespoon corn, safflower or sunflower oil

6 ounces onion, thinly sliced (2 cups)

1/4 cup cider vinegar

1/4 cup water

1 teaspoon sugar

1/2 teaspoon ground cumin or caraway seeds

1 pound Rome Beauty apples, cored, halved and thinly sliced

1/2 teaspoon salt

meatless main courses

Best if prepared at the last minute.

Yield: 2 12-inch pizzas/8 2-slice servings

Crust:

2 packages active dry yeast
(about 1 1/2 tablespoons)

1/2 cup (9 ounces) warm water
(110-115 degrees F.)

1/2 teaspoon sugar

1 pound all-purpose flour
(3 compact cups)

1/2 teaspoon salt

1 1/2 teaspoons corn, safflower or
sunflower oil for greasing pans

Topping:

2 1/2 pounds onions, peeled, and finely
sliced (about 8 cups)

1 cup water

1 tablespoon olive oil

1 teaspoon salt

1 teaspoon freshly ground black pepper

about 3-4 cloves garlic, peeled and
finely chopped (about 2 teaspoons)

2 tomatoes, peeled, seeded and coarsely
chopped (14 ounces)

6 ounces trimmed zucchini, sliced
1/4-inch thick (about 1 cup)

8 ounces trimmed fresh mushrooms,
sliced (about 1 3/4 cups)

5 ounces red bell peppers, cored,
seeded and thinly sliced into rings
(about 1 cup)

5 ounces green bell peppers, cored,
seeded and thinly sliced into rings
(about 1 cup)

4 ounces skim milk mozzarella cheese,
shredded

Provence Pizza

This pizza is particularly good when prepared at the last moment. Depending on your oven, you may have to cook it longer than indicated here to make the dough crisp. It's also important to make the dough thin when shaping it into circles.

To make the crust:

Place yeast, water and sugar in a mixing bowl and stir. Let rest for 5 minutes. Add remaining ingredients and mix with the dough hook of an electric mixer for 3 minutes, or mix by hand for 6 minutes. Knead dough until smooth and satiny.

Place dough in a large bowl and cover the top of the bowl with a towel. Set in a warm place and let rise until double in volume, about 1 hour. (An indentation should remain in the dough when touched with a finger.) While the dough is rising, make the topping.

For the topping:

Place the onions, water, olive oil, salt and pepper in a large kettle and bring to a boil. Boil for approximately 12 minutes or until the water has evaporated. Reduce the heat and continue to cook until the onions are slightly browned, stirring often. Add garlic, mix and set aside.

To assemble the pizza:

After the dough has doubled in volume, divide it into 2 equal pieces. Brush 2 sheet pans with oil and place a ball of dough on each pan. Shape each ball of dough into a 12-inch circle with the edges thicker than the center.

Arrange the tomatoes evenly over the raw dough. Layer with zucchini, mushrooms and peppers. Spread the onion mixture over the vegetables to cover completely.

Top each pizza with 2 ounces of mozzarella cheese.

Bake at 425 degrees for 20 minutes, or until the crust is lightly browned, and serve immediately.

Vegetable topping can be prepared up to a day in advance.

Yield: 8 servings (heaping 1 cup portions)

6 garlic cloves

1 cup fresh cilantro (coriander) loosely packed

3/4 cup water

2 cups broccoli, cut into flowerets

1/2 green pepper, seeded and cut into 1/2-inch dice

1/2 red pepper, seeded and cut into 1/2-inch dice

1 cup fresh mushrooms, 1/2-inch dice

1 cup fresh asparagus, 1/2-inch pieces

1/2 cup celery, 1/4-inch dice

1 cup zucchini, 1/2-inch dice

1/2 cup scallions, sliced

1/2 cup Veal Stock Base Sauce (see page 13)

1 pound angel hair pasta

2 tablespoons olive oil

1/2 teaspoon salt

1/4 cup pine nuts, toasted in a 400-degree oven for 5 minutes

Pasta Primavera

This is an excellent dish. The vegetable mixture can be prepared ahead but the pasta should be cooked at the last moment and tossed with the vegetables just before serving.

Purée the garlic cloves in a food processor with the coriander and 1/4 cup of water.

Heat a large skillet and add the broccoli, green pepper, red pepper, mushrooms, asparagus, celery, zucchini, scallions and the remaining 1/2 cup of water. Cover and cook over medium-high heat for 2 minutes. Remove the lid and cook until the liquid has evaporated.

Add the Veal Stock Base to the puréed garlic-coriander mixture and combine it with the vegetables in the skillet.

Just before serving time, cook the pasta in a pot of boiling water until it is cooked but still slightly firm to the bite (al denté). Drain the pasta and toss with the vegetables, olive oil and salt.

Divide the mixture between 8 individual plates, garnish each serving with 1/2 tablespoon pine nuts and serve immediately.

Tomatoes Stuffed with White Beans

These are excellent done ahead and re-heated or eaten at room temperature. They will develop even more taste a few hours after cooking.

Cut off the smooth end of the tomatoes about 1/4 of the way down and reserve the pieces to use as lids. Scoop out the center flesh and discard the seeds. Chop and reserve the flesh.

Cook the white beans in water to cover, starting them in cold water and cooking them about 1 1/2 hours, until tender. Drain any remaining water.

Combine the rice and the chicken stock in a saucepan, bring to a boil, cover and cook gently for 25 minutes, until the rice is tender.

Combine the cooked beans and rice in a bowl.

Mix together the garlic, ginger and jala-peño pepper. Heat the oil in a skillet and add the garlic mixture. Sauté for about 10 seconds and add the spinach, wet from washing. Continue cooking for 2 minutes, until the spinach is soft and tender.

Add the mixture in the skillet to the beans and rice and stir in the reserved tomato, cumin powder, curry powder and salt. Stuff the tomatoes and place the reserved lids on top.

Arrange the tomatoes in an ovenproof dish and bake in a preheated 400-degree oven for 30 minutes. Serve immediately, serve later reheated, or serve at room temperature.

Yield: 8 servings

8 tomatoes (about 3 1/2 pounds)

8 ounces dry white beans (Navy, Great Northern)

1/2 cup dry white rice

1 cup White Chicken Stock (see page 9)

2 cloves garlic, chopped (1 teaspoon)

1 tablespoon fresh, peeled ginger, chopped

1 teaspoon fresh jalapeño pepper, seeded and chopped

2 tablespoons corn, safflower or sunflower oil

6 ounces fresh spinach, washed just before cooking

1 teaspoon ground cumin

1 teaspoon curry powder

1 teaspoon salt

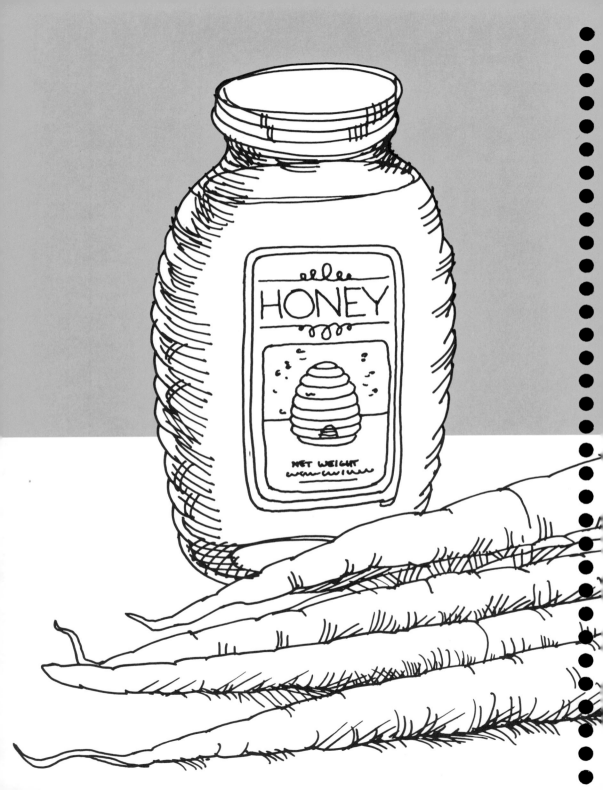

side dishes

Side dishes are used according to season and to one's own taste. For example, dishes like the Hot Rice will complement meat as well as fish but, like the Couscous, Hot Rice is a starchy dish and therefore better in winter than summer. The Potato Salad, Honeyed Sweet Potatoes and Pommes Boulangère are good year-round while the Garlic Broccoli is best in spring and the Roasted Beets best in late summer.

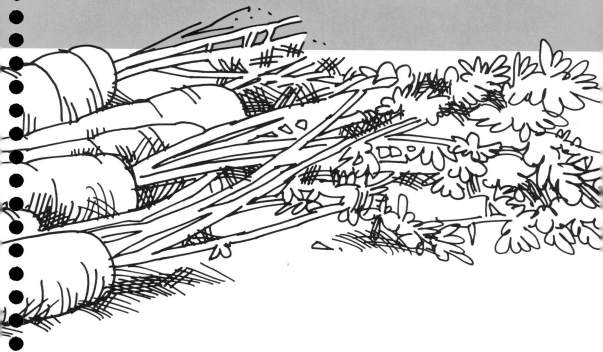

Yield: 6 servings

2 tablespoons corn, safflower or sunflower oil

1 1/2 cups onion, coarsely chopped

1 tablespoon jalapeño pepper, seeded and chopped (decrease or increase quantity depending on degree of hotness desired)

1 tablespoon garlic, chopped (3-5 cloves)

1 teaspoon ground coriander

1 teaspoon ground cumin

1/2 teaspoon ground tumeric

1 1/2 cups long grain rice

3 cups water

Yield: 4 servings

1 tablespoon corn, safflower or sunflower oil

1 cup fast-cooking couscous

1/3 cup raisins

1 cup boiling water

Hot Rice

This is an excellent, spicy side dish.

In a heavy saucepan, combine the oil, onion, jalapeño pepper, garlic, coriander, cumin, and tumeric and cook gently over medium heat for 5 minutes.

Add the rice and mix well. Then, add the water and bring to a boil, stirring occasionally. Cover, reduce the heat to low and cook gently for 20 minutes without stirring. Serve immediately. Note: This is especially good with veal.

Couscous

Couscous, a grainy wheat-base mixture, is excellent with different types of stew, especially lamb. It is easy to prepare, particularly if fast-cooking couscous is used. It cooks in just a few minutes and is flavorful and different.

Heat the oil in a saucepan. When hot, add the couscous and raisins and mix carefully so that all the grains are coated with oil. Pour the boiling water into the pan, cover and let stand 15 minutes at room temperature.

Stir with a fork to separate the grains and serve hot.

Carottes Vichy

Carottes Vichy is a fast dish, always better when done quickly at the last moment so the carrots will have their best nutty, sweet taste.

Place the carrots, oil, water, honey and pepper in a small saucepan, preferably stainless steel. Cover, bring to a strong boil and boil for 5 minutes. Remove the cover, add the garlic and parsley and continue boiling over high heat until most of the liquid has evaporated and the carrots start to sizzle in the little remaining sauce, about 3-4 minutes. Serve immediately.

Yield: 6 servings

2 1/2 cups carrots, peeled and very thinly sliced

1 tablespoon corn, safflower or sunflower oil

1/3 cup water

1 tablespoon honey

1/2 teaspoon freshly ground black pepper

2 cloves garlic, peeled, crushed and chopped very fine (about 1 teaspoon)

3 tablespoons fresh parsley, chopped

Plum Compote

This plum compote is strongly accented with vinegar, sugar, mustard seed, garlic and hot pepper.

Bring both sugars and the vinegar to a boil in a large saucepan.
Add the mustard seed, garlic, onion, pepper flakes, ginger and raisins and return to a boil. Boil for 1 minute and add the plums. Cook the compote until the plums are softened and the syrup is reduced. Let cool to room temperature, cover and refrigerate until ready to use.

Yield: 8 servings

1 cup sugar

1 cup light brown sugar

3/4 cup cider vinegar

2 teaspoons mustard seed

2 cloves garlic, crushed

1/2 cup onion, sliced

2 teaspoons red pepper flakes

1/2 cup slivered ginger

1 cup raisins

3 1/2 cups purple plums, halved and pitted (about 20)

1 pound dry black beans

1 1/2 tablespoons corn, safflower or sunflower oil

1 pound onions, cut into 1-inch cubes

3-5 garlic cloves, chopped (1 tablespoon)

1/2 cup bean liquid (from cooking beans, above)

4 tablespoons chili powder

1/2 teaspoon Tabasco sauce

1 teaspoon ground cumin

3 tomatoes, chopped (1 1/2 cups)

10 scallions, sliced (1 1/2 cups)

1/4 cup white wine vinegar

1/4 teaspoon salt

1/2 cup fresh cilantro (coriander), coarsely chopped

Black Bean Stew

Although this black bean stew has a limited amount of salt and olive oil, it is still quite flavorful and satisfying.

Cook the black beans in water according to package directions.

Drain and reserve 1/2 cup of the cooking liquid.

Heat the oil in a non-stick skillet. When hot, add the onions and sauté 12 minutes or until browned. Add the garlic, black beans and bean liquid and put into a deep saucepan to stew. Add the chili powder, Tabasco and cumin. Cover the pot and boil gently for 10 minutes. Add the tomatoes, scallions, vinegar, salt and cilantro to the beans. Return to a boil and serve immediately.

Onion Papillote

Yield: 4 servings

The Onion Papillote is a very versatile vegetable dish. It is used in this book to make
Onion Sauce (see page 13), but it can also be
served as a vegetable side dish. The cooking
of the peeled onions in the oven will tend to
caramelize them and give them a rich, strong,
filling flavor.

Brush each onion with 1/2 teaspoon of the
oil. Place the onions, stem side up, on a large
piece of aluminum foil. Wrap the foil around
the onions and place the package on a cookie sheet. Bake in the upper third of a preheated 450-degree oven for approximately
60-90 minutes or until the onions are soft and
cooked throughout. Open the foil and turn the
onions over to check that the tops are brown
and caramelized. Serve immediately.

4 8-ounce onions, peeled

2 teaspoons corn, safflower or
sunflower oil

2 bunches very tight broccoli spears
(about 3 pounds total, uncooked, and
2 1/2 pounds, cooked)

2 tablespoons olive oil

3 large garlic cloves, peeled, crushed
and finely chopped (2 teaspoons)

freshly ground black pepper

Garlic Broccoli

This is an excellent dish when the broccoli
is bright green and still crunchy. It is steamed
very fast in a limited amount of water and accented at the last moment with the garlic
cloves and a little olive oil.

Clean and peel the stems of the broccoli
and cut the spears into 1- to 2-inch lengths.

Place 1/2-inch water in a large, shallow
saucepan and bring to a strong boil. Add the
broccoli pieces, cover and boil over high
heat for about 3-4 minutes. Drain.

Heat the oil in a saucepan. When hot, add
the garlic and cook about 10 seconds. Combine with the broccoli and toss with freshly
ground pepper to taste.

Arrange in a serving dish and serve
immediately.

Glazed Turnips

These glazed turnips develop a wonderful, deep, strong, nutty flavor during baking.

Cut the turnips into 1/2-inch slices. Place them in a skillet and cover with 4 cups of boiling water. Boil for 2 minutes, then drain.

Brush a gratin dish with the oil. Arrange the turnips in the dish and sprinkle them with the sugar, pepper and vinegar. Bring the mixture to a boil on top of the stove, then place in a preheated 400-degree oven. Bake for 30 minutes, or until the turnips are soft.

To finish: Brown the turnips for 1-2 minutes under the broiler and serve immediately.

Yield: 6 servings

1 pound turnips, peeled

4 cups boiling water

1 tablespoon corn, safflower or sunflower oil

1 teaspoon sugar

1/8 teaspoon freshly ground black pepper

2 tablespoons vinegar

6 medium-large beets

1 tablespoon olive oil

1 1/2 teaspoons red wine vinegar

Roasted Beets

Beets are always better when roasted in the oven. The aluminum foil tends to concentrate the taste and make them sweet. They are particularly good when new beets are in season.

Cut the tops off the beets and trim at the root ends. Rinse the beets in cold water and wrap them together in a large piece of aluminum foil.

Preheat the oven to 400 degrees and place the foil package on a cookie sheet on the upper rack of the oven. Bake for 90 minutes to 2 hours or until the beets are tender but still firm.

Remove the beets from the foil, cool slightly and peel off the outer skin. Cut the beets into slices and toss with the oil and vinegar while warm.

Serve warm or at room temperature.

Pommes Boulangère

This is a terrific dish that develops even more flavor if made a few hours ahead and reheated. It doesn't dry out and is good to serve with roasted meats or stews.

Cut the potatoes into 1/8-inch slices. Do not rinse after slicing, but put the potatoes directly into a large gratin dish. The potato layer should be about 1 inch thick.

Heat the oil in a skillet, add the onions and sauté about 4 minutes. Add the garlic, bay leaves, thyme, chicken stock and black pepper. Bring the mixture to a strong boil and pour it over the potatoes. Toss the mixture.

Place the potatoes in a preheated 400-degree oven and bake for 60-90 minutes or until the potatoes are soft and the top is well browned. Let the potatoes sit for 20 minutes before serving.

Best if prepared several hours in advance.

Yield: 8 servings

2 pounds peeled potatoes

1 tablespoon corn, safflower or sunflower oil

12 ounces onion, thinly sliced (3 cups)

4-5 cloves garlic, thinly sliced (3 tablespoons)

2 bay leaves

1 teaspoon thyme

3 cups Brown Chicken Stock (see page 10)

1/4 teaspoon freshly ground black pepper

Honeyed Sweet Potatoes

Yield: 8 servings

3 pounds sweet potatoes (about 5), scrubbed and cut crosswise into 1 1/2-inch slices

2 tablespoons corn, safflower or sunflower oil

freshly ground black pepper

3 tablespoons honey

Honeyed sweet potatoes are satisfying and rich, ideal for Thanksgiving or the Christmas holiday season.

Place the sweet potato slices in a saucepan with water to cover. Bring the water to a boil and simmer the potatoes for 5 minutes. Drain.

Heat the oil in a heavy skillet large enough to hold the potatoes in one layer. When hot, add the potatoes, sprinkle with pepper and brown for about 3 minutes on each side.

Add the honey, reduce the heat to low and cook the potatoes, covered, for 5 minutes, turning them once after 2 1/2 minutes.

Serve immediately.

Potato Salad

Potato salad is a must for any type of picnic or outside dining. In this recipe, garlic, scallions and leeks enhance the potatoes and give the dish a wonderful garden flavor.

Heat the oil in a skillet. When hot, add the leeks and sauté 1 minute. Then add the scallions and garlic and sauté 30 seconds longer. Add the wine to the pan and bring to boil. Pour the mixture over the potatoes and add the mustard, pepper and tarragon.

Sprinkle the potatoes with the olive oil, vinegar and sugar. Toss together. Serve warm or cold.

Yield: 8 servings

1 tablespoon corn, safflower or sunflower oil

3/4 cup leeks, finely chopped

5 scallions, sliced (1 cup)

2 teaspoons garlic, chopped

1/3 cup white wine

2 pounds new potatoes, boiled just until cooked through, then sliced

1 tablespoon Dijon mustard

1/2 teaspoon freshly ground black pepper

2 tablespoons fresh tarragon, chopped

5 teaspoons olive oil

2 tablespoons sherry wine vinegar

1 teaspoon sugar

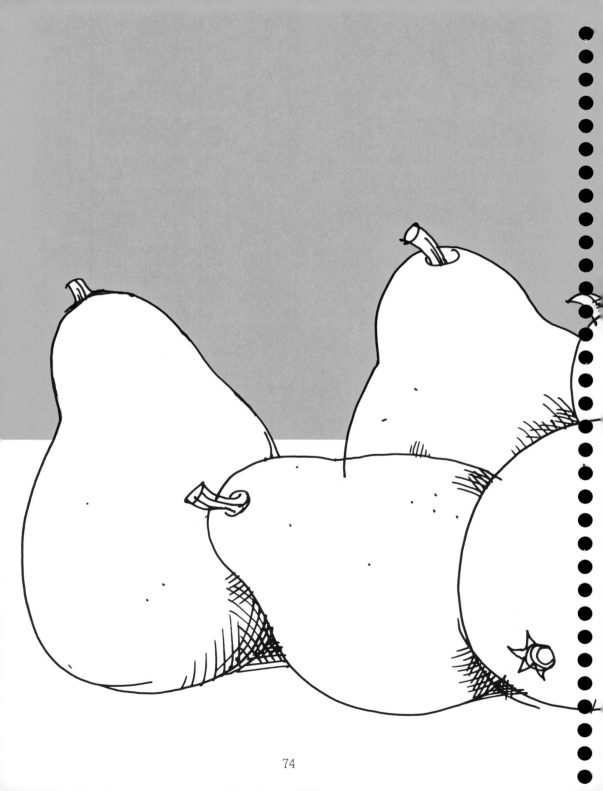

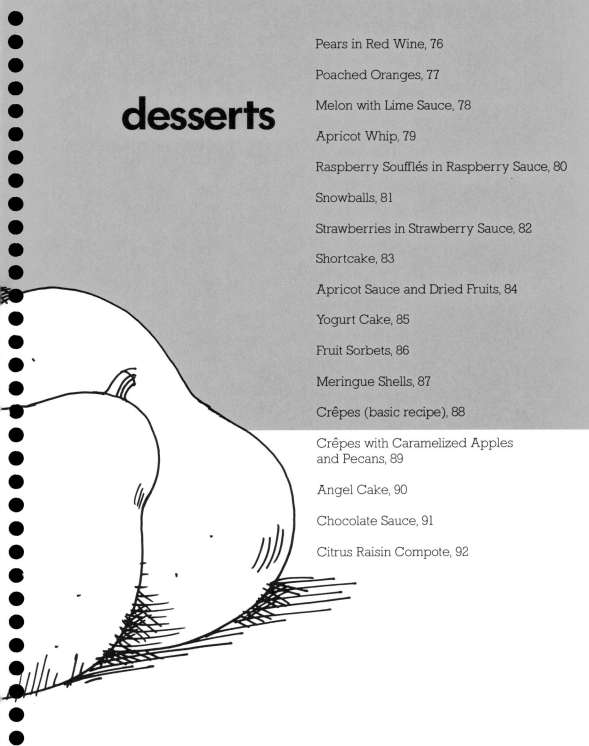

desserts

Yield: 6 servings

4 fairly large Bartlett pears, peeled, quartered and seeded (1 1/2 pounds)

1 1/2 cups hearty red wine

1/3 cup sugar

grated peel of 1 lemon

1/3 cup fresh lemon juice

Pears in Red Wine

The pears in red wine are excellent. The concentrated juice has a beautiful mahogany color and a strong, wine taste. This dessert is particularly good when the pears are in full season, ripe and flavorful.

Combine the pears in a pot with the rest of the ingredients.

Bring to a boil, cover and boil the mixture gently about 25 minutes—less if the pears are very ripe, more if they are hard. You should have approximately 1 1/4 cups of liquid left; if the pears have rendered a lot of juice, you may have more.

Transfer the pears to a bowl. Bring the liquid to a boil and reduce to about 2/3 cup, then combine it with the pears. Cool. The liquid should get syrupy.

Serve in small deep dishes with some of the syrup.

Poached Oranges

Yield: 6 servings

Poached oranges make a good, fast dessert. The oranges have a concentrated taste,
especially with the addition of Grand Marnier,
a brandy flavored with the essential oils of
orange.

Peel the oranges with a sharp knife, removing all the white membrane. Cut the oranges
into 1/2- to 3/4-inch thick slices.

Place the slices in a saucepan with the
sugar and water. Cover, bring to a boil and
simmer gently for 5 minutes.

Carefully remove the orange slices from
the syrup and place them in a serving dish.
Gently boil the syrup to reduce it to approximately 1/3 cup and pour it over the oranges.

When cool or at serving time, sprinkle the
oranges with the Grand Marnier.

6 large seedless oranges

1/3 cup sugar

1/3 cup water

1-2 tablespoons Grand Marnier

Must be prepared at least 1 hour or up to a day in advance.

Yield: 6 servings (2/3 cup each)

4 cups honeydew and/or cantaloupe balls

1 large lime

1 tablespoon rum

1 tablespoon sugar

mint or lime wedges for garnish

Melon with Lime Sauce

The rum and lime make a wonderful sauce for this fast melon dessert.

Cut the melon in half and remove the seeds. Use a melon baller to make the balls and place them in a large bowl.

With a vegetable peeler, remove the green part of the lime skin. Stack the strips of lime together and cut into fine julienne strips. Add the strips to the melon.

Squeeze the lime and mix the juice (approximately 1/3 cup) with the rum and sugar. Stir into the melon.

Allow the mixture to set for 1 hour or as long as 24 hours in the refrigerator.

At serving time, spoon the melon into bowls and garnish with mint or lime wedges.

Apricot Whip

This is a good, light dessert to serve after a rich meal.

Brush a 2-quart baking dish with oil. Coat the bottom and sides of the dish with the 2 tablespoons of sugar.

Place the dried apricots in a saucepan and add enough water to cover. Bring to a boil, reduce heat and cook gently until the apricots are tender when pierced with a fork. Drain the apricots and finely chop them. There should be approximately 1 cup. Mix together the apricots, remaining sugar, vanilla and chopped nuts. Set aside.

Using an electric mixer or a wire whisk, beat the egg whites until stiff. Gently fold the reserved apricot mixture into the egg whites.

Pour the batter into the prepared baking dish and bake in a preheated 375-degree oven for 20-25 minutes, or until lightly browned.

Serve warm or at room temperature.

Yield: 6 servings

1/2 teaspoon corn, safflower or sunflower oil

1/4 cup and 2 tablespoons sugar

5 ounces dried apricots

1 teaspoon pure vanilla extract

1/2 cup coarsely chopped walnuts

5 egg whites

Raspberry Soufflés in Raspberry Sauce

Yield: 12 servings

Raspberry sauce

1 pound fresh raspberries (2 pints)

1/2 cup raspberry jam

Raspberry soufflés

6 egg whites

1/2 cup fresh raspberries

3/4 cup sugar

1 tablespoon corn, safflower or sunflower oil

This is a showy dessert for special parties. Our recipe, using egg whites only with a purée of fresh berries, produces soufflés with a wonderful color and concentrated berry taste.

For the raspberry sauce:

Place raspberries in food processor or blender and purée with the jam; strain. You should have about 2 cups of raspberry sauce.

For the soufflés:

Beat the egg whites with the whisk attachment of the mixer. When the whites are firm, whisk in the sugar. Crush the 1/2 cup of berries in your hand, drop them into the egg whites and fold together. Brush 12 4-ounce soufflé molds lightly with oil and fill the molds with the soufflé mixture. (The mixture should rise above the molds in soft peaks.)

Arrange the filled molds on a cookie sheet and place in a preheated 400-degree oven for 12-15 minutes, until the tops are browned and the soufflés well inflated and firm to the touch.

To serve, coat the bottoms of each of 12 dessert plates with about 1 1/2 to 2 tablespoons of the sauce. Unmold the soufflés by running a sharp knife around the edge and lifting the soufflés out. Place the soufflés browned-side-up on the sauce and drizzle the top of each with an additional 1/2 tablespoon sauce.

Note: This soufflé is also delicious cold.

Snowballs

These are rich cookies that keep well if stored in an airtight container. They can be frozen and defrosted before eating or eaten while still frozen.

Place confectioners' sugar and nuts in a food processor fitted with a metal blade. Blend for 30 seconds, or until the nuts are ground. Place the mixture in a bowl.

Add the egg white and vanilla to the nuts and stir with a spatula to form a paste.

Roll the dough by hand into 1 teaspoon balls and place the balls on an ungreased cookie sheet. Bake in a preheated 325-degree oven for 20 minutes.

Remove from the pan and cool on a wire rack.

Yield: 12 servings

3/4 cup sifted confectioners' sugar

2/3 cup coarsely chopped pecans

1 egg white

1/4 teaspoon pure vanilla extract

Best if prepared several hours in advance.

Yield: 6 servings

2 3/4 cups firm, ripe strawberries, cleaned and stems removed

3 tablespoons strawberry jam

2 teaspoons rum

24 seedless grapes, halved, and mint for garnish

Strawberries in Strawberry Sauce

This is a good combination. The nicest strawberries — left whole or, if very large, halved — are served with a sauce made of imperfect berries. The flavor of this dessert is enhanced greatly if the berries are allowed to develop flavor in the sauce for a few hours before serving.

Cut up enough of the berries (using those that are slightly bruised) to make 3/4 cup and place them in the bowl of a food processor with the jam and rum. Process until smooth.

Combine with the remaining 2 cups of whole strawberries.

To serve, arrange equal portions of the whole berries (tips up) on 6 individual dessert plates. Spoon sauce over the berries and garnish with grapes and mint or serve in equal portions over 6 servings of Shortcake.

Shortcake

A nice, all-purpose shortcake that is excellent served with strawberries in strawberry sauce.

Brush two 8-inch round cake pans with 1/2 teaspoon of the oil. Reserve.

Place the remaining oil, sugar and vanilla in a mixing bowl and mix for 4 minutes or until well blended.

Sift the flour with the baking powder and add the sifted dry ingredients to the sugar-oil-vanilla mixture alternately with the skim milk (beginning and ending with the dry ingredients), beating well after each addition.

Using an electric mixer or a whisk, beat the egg whites until soft peaks form. Reserve.

Gently fold the beaten egg whites into the batter until evenly incorporated.

Divide the batter evenly between the cake pans and bake in a preheated 375-degree oven for 25-30 minutes, or until the cakes test done.

Cool for 10 minutes on a wire rack, then remove the cakes from the pan and finish cooling.

Serve in wedges or cut into circles with a cookie cutter.

Yield: 16 servings

1/2 cup corn, safflower or sunflower oil

1 cup sugar

1 teaspoon pure vanilla extract

2 cups sifted cake flour

1 tablespoon baking powder

3/4 cup evaporated skim milk

3 egg whites, at room temperature

Apricot Sauce and Dried Fruits

Must be prepared at least 1 hour, or up to several weeks in advance.

Yield: 4 servings

1/3 cup honey

1/3 cup lemon juice

3 strips lemon, removed with a vegetable peeler and julienned

3 strips lime, removed with a vegetable peeler and julienned

1/4 cup strained apricot preserves

1/4 cup raisins

1/3 cup dried apricot halves, sliced into strips

8 prunes, cut into 1/2-inch pieces

2 halves dried peaches, sliced into strips

1/4 cup apricot nectar

This apricot sauce with dried fruits can be served with yogurt cake. It can be prepared with the fruits weeks ahead and stored in the refrigerator.

Mix the honey with the lemon juice and julienned lemon and lime rind. Stir in the apricot preserves and nectar. Add the dried fruits and let stand for at least 1 hour.

Yogurt Cake

Good-tasting and moist, this is an excellent basic cake.

Brush an 8-inch round cake pan with about 1/2 teaspoon of the oil and set aside.

Mix the remaining oil, sugar and vanilla together in an electric mixer until well blended. Add the milk and the yogurt and mix. When incorporated, add the sifted flour and baking soda.

Beat the egg whites until stiff and fold them into the batter. Pour the batter into the prepared pan and bake the cake in a preheated 350-degree oven for 20-25 minutes.

Cool to lukewarm and turn the cake out of the pan. Finish cooling. Serve alone or with the Apricot Sauce and Dried Fruits.

Yield: 8 servings

3 tablespoons corn, safflower or sunflower oil

1/2 cup sugar

1 teaspoon pure vanilla extract

1/4 cup skim milk

1/4 cup plain nonfat yogurt

1 cup sifted cake flour

1/2 teaspoon baking soda

2 egg whites

**Can be prepared in advance.
Requires use of commercial
ice cream maker.**

Yield: 4 servings

Simple Syrup

4 cups water

4 cups sugar

Fruit Sorbet

Enough fresh fruit processed in the food
processor to equal 2-3 cups of purée

3/4-1 cup simple syrup

1-2 tablespoons lemon juice

Some suggested proportions:

2 1/2 cups strawberry purée to 3/4 cup
simple syrup to 2 tablespoons
lemon juice

3 cups watermelon purée to 3/4 cup
simple syrup to 1 tablespoon
lemon juice

2 cups pineapple purée to 3/4 cup
simple syrup to 1 tablespoon
lemon juice

2 cups kiwi purée to 1 cup simple syrup
to 1 tablespoon lemon juice

2 cups grapefruit juice to 1 cup simple
syrup (no lemon juice needed)

Fruit Sorbets

Fruit sorbets are excellent do-ahead desserts and can be made with any type of fresh
fruit, which is first processed in a food processor and then combined with a water-sugar
syrup and lemon juice. Strawberries, kiwi,
pineapple and grapefruit all make delicious
sorbet.

Place the water and sugar in a saucepan
and simmer until the sugar is dissolved. Cool
to room temperature, then refrigerate in a
covered jar. Makes 1 generous quart.

Different fruits will require different
amounts of simple syrup and lemon juice to
achieve proper flavor balance. Combine the
fruit purée, syrup and lemon juice. Taste the
mixture and adjust the flavoring to your lik-
ing. Freeze in a commercial ice cream maker
according to the manufacturer's instructions.

Meringue Shells

Can be prepared in advance.

Yield: 15

Meringue shells are always good to have on hand. They can be made weeks ahead and won't get soggy if they are stored in a moisture-proof container. These crisp shells are excellent for fruit sorbets or any of the fruit desserts in the book, from the melon with lime sauce (see page 78) to the strawberries in strawberry sauce (see page 82).

Add a few drops of lemon juice to the egg whites and beat them by hand with a whisk, or by machine (medium to high speed), using a whisk attachment. When the whites hold a nice shape, gradually add 1 cup of sugar and keep beating for 1 minute. The mixture should be stiff and shiny. Fold in the remaining 1/2 cup sugar.

Lightly oil a cookie sheet or use a non-stick cookie sheet.

Fit a pastry bag with a fluted tip and fill with the meringue mixture. Form individual meringue shells by squeezing out 3-inch spirals of meringue to form the base of the shells, then piping a border around the exterior of each base to create a "nest." Bake in a preheated 180- to 190-degree oven for 2 hours or until dry. Let cool.

a few drops lemon juice

6 large egg whites

1 1/2 cups superfine sugar (see page 90)

1 teaspoon corn, safflower or sunflower oil

Can be prepared in advance.

Yield: 24 crêpes

1 cup flour

2/3 cup skim milk

2/3 cup water

4 egg whites

1 tablespoon sugar

1 tablespoon rum

2 tablespoons plus 1/4 teaspoon corn, safflower or sunflower oil

Crêpes
(basic recipe)

Crêpes are very versatile. They can be served as a first course or as a dessert, shaped into a "beggar's purse" (see Crêpe Purse with Mushroom Duxelle, page 22), rolled or folded. Make them ahead and refrigerate or freeze them (securely wrapped) for future use.

Place the flour in a medium-size bowl. Whisk in 1/3 cup of the milk and the egg whites, beating until smooth. Add the remainder of the milk, water, sugar, rum and 2 tablespoons of the oil and whisk until well blended.

Heat an 8-inch non-stick skillet and add the 1/4 teaspoon of oil to the pan (see note below) to coat it. When the oil is hot, place 2 tablespoons of the batter into the skillet and quickly tilt and shake the pan to cover the bottom of the pan with the batter. The faster you spread the batter, the thinner your crêpe will be. Allow the crêpe to cook 35-45 seconds, until browned on the bottom, then turn it over and cook on the other side for an additional 30 seconds. Continue with the remaining batter.

Note: The pan only needs to be oiled once, at the beginning.

Crêpes with Caramelized Apples and Pecans

These crêpes with caramelized apples and pecans should be served lukewarm. The intense flavor resulting from the caramelization of the sugar with the lemon juice, honey and roasted pecan pieces makes this dessert particularly filling and satisfying.

Heat a non-stick skillet and add the sugar and oil. Cook over medium-high heat until the mixture is browned and caramelized, about 1 minute. Add the apple pieces and sauté them about 1 minute.

Mix together the lemon juice, julienned peel, water and honey.

Add to the pan, cover and cook 5 minutes. Remove the cover, add the pecans and cook until the mixture caramelizes, about another 2 minutes.

Fill each of 16 crêpes with 2 tablespoons of the filling. Serve.

Yield: 8 servings/2 crêpes each

3 tablespoons sugar

1 tablespoon corn, safflower or sunflower oil

1 1/2 pounds Red Delicious apples (3-4), cored and cut into 1/2-inch pieces (5 cups)

8 strips of lemon peel, julienned

3 tablespoons lemon juice

1/4 cup water

2 tablespoons honey

1/4 cup pecan pieces

16 crêpes

**Yield: 1 10-inch cake
12 servings/cake**

1 1/4 cups superfine sugar

1 cup sifted confectioners' sugar

1 cup sifted cake flour

1 1/2 cups egg whites (9-10 depending on size)

1 teaspoon almond extract

Angel Cake

This light, airy cake is a classic American dessert. It can be served plain or with chocolate sauce.

Prepare superfine sugar by placing granulated sugar in a food processor fitted with a metal blade. Turning the machine off and on a few times, process the sugar until it is very fine. Set aside.

Combine the confectioners' sugar and cake flour. Sift and reserve.

In a very large bowl, combine the egg whites and almond extract. Beat on high speed of an electric mixer until the whites form peaks when the beater is lifted. Add the superfine sugar, a small amount at a time, beating only long enough after each addition to incorporate the sugar.

Using a spatula, carefully fold the flour mixture, a spoonful at a time, into the egg white mixture, making sure all the flour is incorporated. Do not overmix.

Pour the batter into an ungreased 10-inch tube pan. Bake in the center of a preheated 350-degree oven for 35 minutes, or until the cake springs back when lightly touched.

Invert the pan on an overturned funnel or over a cake rack. Allow to hang until the cake is cold. To remove the cake from the pan, run a sharp, thin-bladed knife around the sides of the pan with a steady stroke. Invert onto a serving plate.

Chocolate Sauce

Yield: 1/2 cup sauce/4 servings

This is a strong, concentrated chocolate sauce made with cocoa. It goes well with the angel cake or other cakes.

Bring the water and sugar to a boil in a saucepan and boil for 1 minute. Mix in the cocoa, whisk until well blended, and strain into a container. The sauce will thicken as it cools. Store in the refrigerator; warm sauce before serving.

1/3 cup water

1/3 cup sugar

1/3 cup cocoa (preferably Dutch)

Citrus Raisin Compote

Yield: 8 servings

1/2 medium-sized grapefruit, seeded and cut into 1/4-inch slices (about 1 cup)

2 medium-sized oranges, halved, seeded and sliced into 1/4-inch slices (about 2 1/2 cups)

1 large lime, halved, seeded and sliced into 1/4-inch slices (about 3/4 cup)

3/4 cup sugar

1/2 cup dark raisins

1 tablespoon cognac or rum

mint garnish

This compote can be used as a side dish or condiment with meat or poultry. It also makes a delicious dessert, alone or with angel cake (see page 90) or yogurt cake (see page 85). With the cooked citrus fruit slices, it has a highly accented flavor and a little goes a long way. It should be served very cold.

Place the fruits in a saucepan, preferably stainless steel, and cover generously with water. Bring to a boil and let boil for about 10-15 seconds to eliminate some of the fruits' bitterness. Pour into a colander, discarding the liquid, and rinse under cold water.

Return the fruit to the saucepan with the sugar and 4 cups of water. Bring to a boil and boil gently, uncovered, for 50 minutes. Skim off any impurities that come to the surface, especially during the first 1/2 hour of cooking. After 50 minutes, add the raisins and continue to cook for another 10 minutes. (There will be liquid to baste and wet the fruit.)

Let cool to room temperature, cover and refrigerate until ready to use. When cool, add the cognac or rum and serve, garnished with fresh mint.

Suggested Menus

Below are sample menus that can be created using recipes from this book. Remember, your menus may include any combination of an hors d'oeuvre, soup, salad, main course, side dish and dessert.

Cold Peach Soup
Navarin of Lamb
Angel Cake with Chocolate Sauce

Egg Whites Stuffed with Bulgar
Chicken Stir-Fry
Crêpes with Caramelized Apples and
Pecans

Vegetable Soup with Basil Pistou
Pepper Steak
Pommes Boulangère
Raspberry Soufflés in Raspberry Sauce

Jalapeño Dip
Pasta Primavera
Strawberry Shortcake

Crêpe Purse with Mushroom Duxelle
Sea Scallops Grenobloise
Poached Oranges

Gazpacho
Sautéed Veal Chops with Vegetables
Hot Rice
Apricot Whip

Oatmeal Soup
Sole Fillets with Stewed Tomatoes
Garlic Broccoli
Pears in Red Wine

Salad with Creamy Cucumber Dressing
Turkey Cassoulet
Plum Compote
Snowballs

Ratatouille Dip
Pork Tenderloin with Apples and Onions
Carottes Vichy
Fruit Sorbet

Salad with Vinaigrette Dressing
Provence Pizza
Yogurt Cake with Apricot Sauce

Salad with Creamy French-Style Dressing
Chicken African-Style
Couscous
Citrus Raisin Compote

Vegetable Soup with Basil Pistou
Blackened Swordfish
Potato Salad
Melon with Lime Sauce

One of the special advantages of cooking with **A Fare for the Heart** is that you **don't** have to follow charts. All of the recipes are created to fit heart-healthy guidelines for dinner, regardless of what combination of dishes you choose to serve.

However, for those who are curious at heart, we have included a nutritional breakdown of each dish per serving. Goals have been set in each food category for maintaining an acceptable level of fat, cholesterol and sodium. These figures are the numbers listed in the color bar to the right of each section.

Nutritional Profiles

	Fat grams	Cholesterol milligrams	Sodium milligrams	Calories
Soups	**4.0**	**5**	**150**	**—**
Cold Peach Soup	0.3	0	7	207
Gazpacho	1.9	0	93	65
Oatmeal Soup	3.8	4	128	84
Vegetable Soup with Basil Pistou	1.0	2	104	78
Hors d'oeuvre	**7.5**	**0**	**200**	**—**
Crêpe Purse with Mushroom Duxelle	6.9	0	207	131
Egg Whites Stuffed with Bulgar	0.3	0	178	107
Jalapeño Dip	4.2	0	149	90
Ratatouille Dip with Endive	2.4	0	192	112
Salad Dressings	**5.0**	**0**	**100**	**—**
Creamy Cucumber Dressing	1.7	0	78	31
Creamy French-Style Dressing	2.6	0	70	31
Vinaigrette Dressing	3.6	0	98	40
Main Courses	**20.0**	**100**	**500**	**—**
Fish				
Blackened Swordfish	7.8	75	123	160
Fillet of Sole in Salad Casing	8.2	68	355	261

	Fat grams	Cholesterol milligrams	Sodium milligrams	Calories
Salmon with Sorrel Sauce	4.8	45	345	187
Sea Scallops Grenobloise	5.7	60	451	206
Sole Fillets with Stewed Tomatoes	4.2	85	326	151
Poultry				
Chicken African-Style	13.0	89	289	288
Chicken in Mustard Sauce	5.5	64	217	207
Chicken Sauce Piquant	8.2	62	365	233
Chicken Stir-Fry	10.1	51	501	258
Turkey Cassoulet	5.2	64	277	317
Meats				
Carbonnade of Beef	9.8	80	452	255
Lamb Steak in Sweet Piquant Sauce	9.0	74	443	197
Marinated Flank Steak	8.7	62	414	211
Navarin of Lamb	10.4	76	397	290
Pepper Steak	14.9	87	334	316
Pork Tenderloin with Apples and Onions	7.8	72	299	259
Sautéed Veal Chops with Vegetables	20.4	101	331	325
Meatless Main Courses				
Pasta Primavera	7.8	0	172	312
Provence Pizza	6.1	8	445	359
Tomatoes Stuffed with White Beans	4.4	0	281	203
Side Dishes	**5.0**	**0**	**150**	—
Black Bean Stew	4.4	0	110	262
Carottes Vichy	2.4	0	45	62
Couscous	4.3	0	7	347
Garlic Broccoli	5.0	0	20	98

	Fat grams	Cholesterol milligrams	Sodium milligrams	Calories
Glazed Turnips	2.3	0	38	37
Honeyed Sweet Potatoes	3.9	0	22	232
Hot Rice	5.0	0	5	227
Onion Papillote	2.6	0	2	58
Plum Compote	0.2	0	17	310
Pommes Boulangère	2.1	0	152	143
Potato Salad	4.8	0	35	162
Roasted Beets	2.3	0	24	36
Desserts	**7.5**	**0**	**100**	**—**
Angel Cake	0.1	0	42	149
Apricot Sauce and Dried Fruits	0.4	0	9	350
Apricot Whip	6.4	0	44	181
Chocolate Sauce	1.3	0	52	78
Citrus Raisin Compote	0.1	0	1	121
Crêpes with Caramelized Apples and Pecans	6.6	0	23	178
Fruit Sorbets	0.4	0	3	216
Melon with Lime Sauce	0.3	0	9	54
Meringue Shells	0.3	0	20	81
Pears in Red Wine	0.4	0	7	154
Poached Oranges	0.2	0	trace	117
Raspberry Soufflés in Raspberry Sauce	1.4	0	26	122
Shortcake	7.0	trace	87	162
Snowballs	4.1	0	4	66
Strawberries in Strawberry Sauce	0.7	0	3	108
Yogurt Cake	5.3	trace	73	144

Helpful Hints

Fresh is always your best choice, followed by frozen and canned. Be sure to read all labels to avoid salt and additives.

Add fresh herbs and salt at the end of a recipe to achieve maximum flavor.

Use heavy-weight, non-stick pans to simplify your cooking.

Place a gratin dish or a soufflé pan on a cookie sheet for better heat transfer and easier handling.

For best searing results, preheat your skillet before sautéeing.

To test meat for doneness, press it with your fingers. The more resilient the meat, the more well done it is.

Heavy aluminum pans give the best heat transfer for sautéeing meats and vegetables. Stainless steel pans are best for cooking with liquids.

When cooking a variety of vegetables together, cut the quicker-cooking vegetables into larger pieces.

Break raw eggs on a flat surface to avoid breaking the yolk. Put the eggs into a bowl and separate by lifting the yolks out with your hands. This is easiest if the eggs are cold.

Beat egg whites while still cool for the correct texture.

When straining raspberry sauce, tap the side of the strainer with a spoon to release the juice. Do not press the seeds through the strainer.

Seeds from the strained raspberries can be added to vinegar to make raspberry vinegar.

To skin ripe tomatoes easily, drop them into boiling water for about 20 seconds, then immediately plunge into ice water and peel.

Rinse cut onions in a sieve under cold water for milder flavor.

Undercook meats and fish slightly if they will rest before serving. They will finish cooking through their own residual heat.

A stir-fry is a good way to use up small amounts of vegetables in your refrigerator.

Sorbets are an excellent way to use up over-ripened fruit.

About The Cleveland Clinic Foundation

The Cleveland Clinic Foundation is a National Referral Center and an international health resource dedicated to providing excellent specialized medical care in response to public need. The Foundation is recognized worldwide for its comprehensive commitment to understanding, controlling and preventing diseases of the heart and circulatory system, including:

Major discoveries linking high blood pressure to atherosclerosis.

Understanding the role of cholesterol in cardiovascular disease.

Development of coronary angiography to detect life-threatening obstructions in the coronary arteries.

First successful use of a powerful, genetically engineered drug, t-PA, in dissolving blood clots in the limbs.

Pioneered bypass surgery, including the use of internal mammary artery grafts which have increased patients' ten-year survival rates from 88% to 93%.

To make an appointment at The Cleveland Clinic Foundation, please call 444-5641 in Cleveland, or toll-free 1-800-362-2306 (in Ohio) or 1-800-321-5398 (outside of Ohio). Hearing impaired individuals may call TTY: (216) 444-0261.

Order Form

VHS Video and Cookbook

Please send me [ ] copies of **A Fare for the Heart** VHS video/cookbooks at $39.95 each.

Residents of Ohio please add $2.80 sales tax per set.

Shipping and handling $4.00 per set.

Cookbook only

Please send me [ ] copies of **A Fare for the Heart** cookbooks at $9.95 each.

Residents of Ohio please add $.70 sales tax per book.

Shipping and handling $2.00 per book.

Total enclosed

Please send ordered books/videos to:

_____
Name (Please print)

_____
Street

_____
City   State   Zip Code

VHS **A Fare for the Heart** video/cookbook sets are available by mail or phone. Video features Chef Jacques Pepin demonstrating recipes from the **A Fare for the Heart** cookbook and heart-healthy hints from Cleveland Clinic Foundation specialists. Cookbooks also sold separately.

$ _____

$ _____

$ _____

$ _____

$ _____

$ _____

$ _____

Make checks payable to **The Cleveland Clinic Foundation** and mail your orders to:
The Cleveland Clinic Foundation
10465 Carnegie Avenue
Cleveland, Ohio 44106

Please allow four weeks for order processing and shipping.

Visa and MasterCard orders accepted. Please call **1-800-258-8787, extension 240**.

About Jacques Pepin

Jacques Pepin, renowned cookbook author and teacher, was born in 1935 in Bourg-en-Bress, France, into a family of restaurateurs. He was personal chef to three French presidents, including Charles de Gaulle, and was chef at the famous Plaza Athenee in Paris.

Pepin moved to the United States in 1959. He now appears regularly on radio and television and conducts cooking classes across the country and Canada.

He was a consultant for "Classic French Cooking" in Time Life's series of "Foods of the World," and has authored seven of his own cookbooks. He is currently a contributor to many major culinary magazines.